World War II
Veterans in Motorsports

World War II Veterans in Motorsports

Art Evans

McFarland & Company, Inc., Publishers
Jefferson, North Carolina

Library of Congress Cataloguing-in-Publication Data

Names: Evans, Arthur G., author.
Title: World War II veterans in motorsports / Art Evans.
Description: Jefferson, North Carolina : McFarland & Company, Inc., Publishers, [2019] | Includes bibliographical references and index.
Identifiers: LCCN 2019003385 | ISBN 9781476676708 (paperback : acid free paper) ∞
Subjects: LCSH: Automobile racing drivers—United States—Biography. | Motorsports—United States—History—20th century. | World War, 1939-1945—Veterans—Biography.
Classification: LCC GV1032.A1 E83 2019 | DDC 796.720922 [B] —dc23
LC record available at https://lccn.loc.gov/2019003385

British Library cataloguing data are available

ISBN (print) 978-1-4766-7670-8
ISBN (ebook) 978-1-4766-3590-3

© 2019 Art Evans. All rights reserved

No part of this book may be reproduced or transmitted in any form or by any means, electronic or mechanical, including photocopying or recording, or by any information storage and retrieval system, without permission in writing from the publisher.

Front cover: Sam Hanks, winner of the 1946 Pacific Coast Midget Championship (courtesy of Alice Hanks)

Printed in the United States of America

McFarland & Company, Inc., Publishers
Box 611, Jefferson, North Carolina 28640
www.mcfarlandpub.com

Acknowledgments

The most important contributors to this book are John and Ginny Dixon. They not only reviewed the manuscript but also looked up histories and checked facts. John also wrote some passages. This book would not have been possible without them; they are dear friends. Lots of thanks to Dylan Lightfoot, assistant editor at McFarland, for his expertise and suggestions. He made this book much better than it was when I first proposed it. Jaime Chamberlain, son of Jay Chamberlain, filled in Jay's military experience. Alice Hanks provided first-person information about her husband, Sam, and allowed me to use some photographs she has in her collection. Jim Peterson's son, Steve, filled me in on many details I didn't know about his dad plus his military history. Thanks to Dr. Ernest Nagamatsu for his input regarding Max Balchowsky. Thanks to Larry Berman, who has collected a large number of photographs of John Fitch. Thanks to Ginny Sims, who gave a lot of information and photographs about her best friend, Mary Davis, and herself. Thanks to Tracey Smith, executive vice president of Shelby American, who helped with the chapter on Carroll. Thanks to Peter Miles, Ken's son, for his input regarding his father. Thanks also to Rex McAfee for information on his father, Jack, and Willie Stroppe, son of Bill Stroppe. I want to express my thanks to Bernard Cahier, Bob D'Olivo, Dave Friedman, Ron Kellogg, Allen Kuhn, Lester Nehamkin, Rod Bean, Doug Stokes, Ron Cummings and Jim Sitz, all of whom contributed in one way or another. Unfortunately, some are no longer with us.

Table of Contents

Acknowledgments v
Prologue 1

1. John Fitch   5
2. Ed Hugus   15
3. Paul Newman   21
4. Mary Davis   27
5. Bill Devin   35
6. Jay Chamberlain   41
7. Jack McAfee   49
8. Ken Miles   57
9. Jim Peterson   66
10. Vasek Polak   72
11. Bill Pollack   79
12. Carroll Shelby   87
13. John Von Neumann   100
14. Rodger Ward   107
15. Sam Hanks   115
16. Steve McQueen   124
17. Ginny Sims   129
18. Shav Glick   137
19. Chuck Daigh   142
20. Bill Stroppe   150
21. Pete Lovely   158
22. Max Balchowsky   166
23. Dan Gurney   175

Epilogue   185
Bibliography   187
Index   189

Prologue

This book is written in the first person. I have done so because all of the 23 people in it are (or were) my friends, some very close ones. So when you read "I," "me" or "mine," I refer to myself.

The term "the Greatest Generation" was made popular by the renowned journalist Tom Brokaw in his excellent 1998 book of that title. His book describes those who grew up in the United States during the deprivation of the Great Depression and went on to serve during World War II. Brokaw wrote, "It is, I believe, the Greatest Generation any society has ever produced." President Franklin Delano Roosevelt said, "This generation of Americans has a rendezvous with destiny."

Brokaw went on to write, "The young Americans of this time constituted a generation birth-marked for greatness, a generation of Americans that would take its place in American history. They were involved in a tumultuous journey through adversity and achievement, despair and triumph."

During World War II, the average age of the 23 men and women I depict in this book was 20. Some were only teenagers. Two of them, Ken Miles and Vasek Polak, were not Americans during the war but later became citizens. At least one, Carroll Shelby, not only was a great racing driver but also created cars that are still manufactured. Two others, John Von Neumann and Vasek Polak, were instrumental in helping to establish Porsche as a marque in the United States. John Fitch, Ed Hugus, Chuck Daigh, Bill Stroppe, Max Balchowsky, Jay Chamberlain, Jim Peterson and Paul Newman were true heroes in the war. Others left their marks on businesses and motorsports.

The 1950s saw a new type of sport: the emergence of amateur sports-car road racing in the United States. Some call it "the Fabulous Fifties," and the Greatest Generation who went racing were significant in its creation. Having encountered sports cars, especially MGs, in England, many American servicemen were hooked on these small, nimble two-seaters. Some brought an MG home, while others acquired one in another way. So the first post-war sports-car road races in the United States were dominated by MGs.

The guys and gals who raced, flagged and wrenched during the fifties were pursuing their passion on weekends. The first courses were on public streets and roads. Unlike most other amateur sports, with the exception of some school football, baseball and basketball games, sports-car races often attracted large crowds of spectators and were covered in newspapers and magazines.

When road racing in the United States started after World War II, for the most part, events were operated by the Sports Car Club of America (SCCA). The California Sports Car Club (Cal Club) in Southern California was another organizing body. Both clubs had rather strict rules regarding professionalism. If a member—and only members could drive in club races—accepted prize money for racing, the member was not allowed to enter a club event for a year afterwards.

Amateurism, however, didn't apply to those few SCCA members who were paid, under the table as it were, by private entrants. As an example, Carroll Shelby's car owner-entrant was most often John Edgar, a wealthy sportsman who wanted his cars to win. Rodger Ward told the story that one day he was talking with Shelby and noted that if Shel would turn professional in the United States, he could earn some significant money. Shelby asked Ward how much. When Ward replied, Shelby said, "Oh, I couldn't afford that!" If Shelby ran as a U.S. professional, he couldn't run with the SCCA. In addition, amateurism didn't apply to club members who raced and accepted prize money at events outside the United States. Shelby started racing professionally in Europe for Aston Martin in 1954 while racing as an amateur with the SCCA in the United States.

The 12 Hours of Sebring was an exception. From the beginning, Sebring was organized by a professional promoter, Alec Ulmann. The first Sebring race took place on December 31, 1950. Ulmann's idea all along was to create an international endurance race. That first race, however, was for only six hours and, because Alec applied too late, there was no professional sanction from the American Automobile Association (AAA) or the FIA (Federation International de L'Automobile). Ultimately the event was sanctioned by the SCCA and was amateur only. Even dealing with a professional promoter ruffled some SCCA feathers.

For 1953, Ulmann lengthened the airport race to 12 hours, opened it to professionals and offered prize money. The SCCA would have none of it, so Alec obtained a sanction from the AAA, and the FIA made it part of the new World Sports Car Championship, which had been inaugurated only five weeks previously. Sebring became the first event in the international series.

Briggs Cunningham entered John Fitch and Phil Walters in his 5.4-liter Cadillac-powered Cunningham C4R. Up against Briggs were two factory-entered Aston Martins plus a number of privately entered Ferraris and Jaguars. From the start, it was a duel between the Cunningham and the Astons. For most of the first six hours, the Astons led, but towards the middle, the C4R pulled in front and took the checkered flag. Reg Parnell and George Abecassis were second in an Aston. Fitch and Walters had the honor of winning the very first World Sports Car Championship event.

The event that truly transformed American road racing, however, was the first U.S. Grand Prix for Sports Cars at Riverside on October 12, 1958. It was sanctioned by the U.S. Auto Club (USAC) and the FIA, AAA having bowed out after the 1955 Le Mans disaster. USAC had established the USAC Road Racing Championship series. Initiated in 1958, the series continued through the 1962 season. Competition was for sports-racing prototypes and paid prize money although sometimes not very much. USAC was able to put together only four events that first year, so initially, the series was rather anemic.

Unlike the first three 1958 events, the last race of the season was a big deal, perhaps enough to save the series. What made it such a huge success was the promotion of the powerful *Los Angeles Times*. Previously, racing had received sometimes meager press attention. Sports pages were filled with baseball and football. But that changed with the *Times* involved.

American and a few European professionals—Jo Bonnier, Roy Salvadori and Jean Behra—mixed with the usual Cal Club and SCCA amateurs to form a field of 46 entrants. Stirling Moss planned on coming but had to renege because of a Formula One conflict. Indy winners Jim Rathmann, Troy Ruttman and Johnny Parsons were joined by superstars Bobby Unser and Rodger Ward. The usual sports-car front-runners were there, including Carroll Shelby, John Von Neumann, Dan Gurney and Ken Miles. And lo and behold, neither the SCCA nor the Cal Club set down any of its members for running the race.

When the flag dropped for the 200-mile event, local Southern Californians were in front. Chuck Daigh and Lance Reventlow each led off in Lance's new Scarab. Phil Hill, John Von Neumann, Dan Gurney and Richie Ginther drove Ferraris, followed by Max Balchowsky in his Old Yeller Buick-powered special. The pros from both Europe and the United States faded fast. Chuck and Lance led the way followed by Hill, Von Neumann, Gurney and Ginther. Hill passed Lance and then Phil and Chuck put on a spirited show until Hill's engine got vapor lock. Chuck took the checker, watched by over 100,000 spectators, and the Scarab marque became something to reckon with, virtually right out of the box.

In July 1959, the SCCA started to bend. The Kiwanis Club sponsored another Grand Prix for sports cars at Riverside on July 19, 1959. It was a first. The previously amateur-only SCCA jointly sanctioned it, along with the professional USAC. The SCCA promulgated a new rule that permitted its members to drive in professional events so long as they did not accept any prize money. The day was very hot—100-plus degrees—so there were only about 26,000 spectators. Richie Ginther won in a Von Neumann Ferrari followed by five Porsche 550 Spyders.

Not to be outdone by the USAC, the SCCA organized its own fully professional U.S. Road Racing Championship. The first event took place in 1963. Meanwhile, the USAC series was fading and abandoned after the 1962 season. The SCCA reorganized itself into two parts, professional and amateur, as it remains today. Vintage racing has, of course, remained amateur with no prize money offered. Professionals may enter, however, and sometimes do. Bobby Unser, for instance, raced my Devin SS one time in a vintage event.

1
John Fitch

John Fitch was a most unusual man. Until later in the fifties, he was one of the very few Americans of international road racing caliber. His life is the stuff of legend.

John burst on the world scene in early 1951 at the General Peron Grand Prix. (The first Argentine Grand Prix, for sports cars). A number of leading European teams of the time were joined by a few Americans, North and South. John borrowed a car and won.

John Cooper Fitch was born in Indianapolis on August 4, 1917. He is descended from the John Fitch who invented the steamboat (although Robert Fulton received the credit). John's parents divorced in 1923. When John was six, his mother married George Spindler, then president of Stutz and a sometime factory race driver. John remembered holding on for dear life to the seat of a Bearcat while his stepfather drove around the Indianapolis Speedway.

"I wanted to see the world," Fitch said. "So I asked my parents to send me to the Kentucky Military Institute, a school in faraway Kentucky." Even more appealing, the school had taken over several hotels when the real estate bubble burst in Florida and moved there for a semester each year. "That was the big attraction," he added.

Next John entered Lehigh University to study civil engineering because the Fitch family business was road paving. He didn't stay long. Instead he bought an Indian Twin and rode it to New Orleans where he met a man who owned a Fiat Topolino and was willing to trade even up for the motorcycle.

In 1939 he boarded a tramp steamer to England with the idea of riding a horse from Paris to Rome. This trip, John thought, would be the ideal way to soak up the culture of the two nations as well as learn languages. But his application for a visa to France was turned down because of the impending war. John liked the theater, and that was where he met a young and beautiful ballet dancer. They became a couple. She introduced him to a Ham Johnson. John and Ham pooled their resources and bought a used MG Magnette, a small sedan, in which they toured the British Isles. John and Ham were arrested in York. The police thought John was a spy because he had been taking countless pictures, including shots of some military vehicles. The two men remained in the clink until John's film was developed and showed he was not a spy. After the tour, John returned to the United States.

As war approached, the outlook was grim. John told me, "I decided I'd do something I had always wanted to do." With a small inheritance from his grandfather, he bought a 32-foot schooner he named the *Banshee*. Then he latched onto a winsome first mate and spent nearly a year cruising the Gulf of Mexico. After World War II started in Europe, German submarines lurked near our shores looking for ships to sink.

John joined a group of small boaters the Coast Guard had organized to spot and report the locations of subs. He failed to spot any, but the first mate was to play an important part later in his life.

Knowing that war was on the way for the United States, John joined the Army in 1940. His exploits and adventures as an Air Corps pilot are legendary in and of themselves. He was among the first group of Americans to arrive in England early in 1942 who flew bombers over Europe and then North Africa. During this tour, he flew over 100 missions.

After North Africa, Fitch was sent to Wright Field (now Wright-Patterson Air Force Base) to serve as a test pilot. His first job was testing a B-25 that had been converted into what was hoped to be a tank killer. A 75 mm cannon (without the caisson) was fitted with a recoil device and installed in the aircraft. The pilot was also the aimer. The idea was to point the plane at a tank and fire the cannon. Floating targets were placed in nearby Lake Erie, and John flew and fired until the device was perfected. Subsequently, the 75 mm–equipped B-25 was employed in the Pacific Theater.

His next assignment was testing the maximum speed possible with a P-51. When

John Fitch with his first mate, Matilda, on his schooner, the *Banshee*, off the coast of Florida. In 1939, Fitch used it to look for German submarines. John Fitch collection.

John and his crew flew more than 100 missions over Europe in 1942. In 1944, he flew a P-51 fighter to support the invasion of Germany. He is shown at left with his crew in 1942. John Fitch collection.

the plane was flown at full throttle, overheating would cause the engine to soon fail. A water injection device was installed. Sam Hanks worked on the development of this device. John's task was to fly at 35,000 feet with full throttle until the engine blew. Then he had to make a dead-stick landing. He kept at this until the device was fully developed. During his time at Wright Field, his *Banshee* first mate visited, and they resumed their affair.

After returning to the European theater, John was assigned to the famous Eagle Squadron based in England. He flew P-51s escorting bombers to Germany. In 1944 he shot down an ME 262. He caught it when it was climbing out after taking off from a hidden spot on the autobahn. This German jet was much faster than John's P-51 Mustang, so bagging it was a most unusual feat. He flew more than 50 missions in the P-51.

By the end of 1944, there was no more Luftwaffe to threaten the bombers, so the fighter pilots were redirected towards shooting at ground targets. In January 1945, John was trying to destroy a train locomotive. He made the mistake of making a second pass and was hit by anti-aircraft fire and had to jump. As he bailed out, he was hit by the tail and injured. He and his parachute landed near the burning aircraft. Soon, members of the German Home Guard arrived with pitchforks and axes looking to kill the pilot. John managed to hide under some nearby brush, and eventually the Germans gave up the search.

John had an escape kit that included a compass. When night came, he started walking towards the Allied lines many hundreds of miles away. Wearing his American flight suit, he knew he couldn't walk during daylight hours. When dawn broke, he hid in the loft of a barn and went to sleep. The next morning, he was wakened by the farmer who invited him into the farmhouse where the wife prepared breakfast for John. (By then, most Germans knew the war was lost.) During his time at the farm, he became acquainted with the couple as well as the farmer's daughter.

Eventually, the townspeople learned about the American pilot and John was taken to the city hall. The mayor wanted to kill John and struck him. But the members of the city council objected, and John was turned over to German military authorities. He was transported with some other prisoners through Nuremberg, which had been virtually destroyed and was still being bombed. The group with their guards narrowly escaped being hit.

When John finally arrived in the Luftwaffe prison camp, he was questioned by German soldiers to find out if he had any information that might be useful. The sessions were lengthy and there were two interrogators, a good guy and a bad guy, both of whom, of course, spoke English. The bad guy was harsh, but there was no physical torture. Eventually, the good guy revealed that he had lived in New Orleans before the war, but when the war started he returned to Germany to serve. It turned out the good guy had a close friend in New Orleans and, incredibly, this was the same person to whom Fitch had sold his sailboat in 1940. After that, a sort of friendship developed between the two. Eventually the man broke down, almost in tears, and confessed he had made a terrible mistake by returning to Germany. He had been happy and prosperous in New Orleans. He said that, now, all was lost; that he was as ruined as Germany.

In the spring, General George Patton's Seventh Army was approaching the prison camp and the guards fled. Fitch had not taken a shower for months, as there were no facilities for prisoners. After the guards left, he and some others went to the guards' quarters and took showers. While they were there, General Patton came in and greeted each one personally. John remembered the incident well. "I was stark naked when I met General Patton." Finally, the general said, "Now I have to go and kill some more Germans."

Shortly after his discharge, John went to Florida and started a small seaplane charter service. Through a mutual friend, he was invited to a party at the Kennedy compound. He met Joe and Rose's daughter, Kathleen, and they started to date. When Joe was the ambassador to the United Kingdom, Kathleen had met and married Lord Harrington. When he was killed in combat, she returned to the States.

For much of the rest of the decade, John was intimately involved with the Kennedy family. It took some years for me to get the entire story out of him, but little by little, details came out. It's a part of history, and I think it's important to preserve.

1. John Fitch

John with Rose Kennedy during a fishing trip off the coast of Florida in 1946. Photograph by Kathleen Kennedy. John Fitch collection.

John described Kathleen as tall and athletic. She had an Irish sense of humor and was very perceptive regarding others' feelings. Still and all, as the daughter of a U.K. ambassador and widow of an English Lord, she was very much a part of the jet set. John's dates with Kathleen included not only parties and dinners but also less formal occasions such as the fishing excursion pictured here. The photo of John and Rose, taken by Kathleen, and another photo were the only memorabilia John retained of that time in his collection.

Fitch recalled Joe Kennedy as a rather crude individual who flaunted his much younger girlfriends in front of his family, including Rose. John really liked Rose, who, he says, was a warm personality. He thinks it took great fortitude to put up with Joe. But it was a Catholic marriage, which in those days didn't accept divorce.

JFK (called Jack by his friends) and Teddy were around too, but Bobby wasn't in Florida much. John remembered Teddy as a fat and obnoxious kid. He told me he didn't think the senator had improved his personality much since then.

One particular party at the compound stuck in John's memory. There were a great many guests, and John had to relieve himself. Finding a long line at the facilities, he repaired to a remote and secluded bush in the garden. While doing his duty on one side of the bush, he spied another guest doing the same on the other side: the former king of England!

As two veterans of similar ages, Jack and John became friends. Naturally they exchanged war stories. Jack was recuperating in Florida from injuries to his back sustained when his PT boat was sunk. John had been injured when he bailed out and was burned when he landed. John recalled one particular conversation while they were lounging around the pool. They were wondering what they would do for the rest of their lives. John noted that Jack would never have to worry about making a living. Politics of the day, particularly in Massachusetts, was a rather dirty business. John suggested that Jack, without the need for money, could make a significant contribution.

After Kathleen was killed in a plane crash in 1949, John moved to White Plains, New York, and opened a foreign-car repair shop. He entered his first race in an MGTC in June 1949 at Bridgehampton. Then he entered the first Sebring in his XK120 Jaguar on December 31, 1950.

John's first international race was in an American stock car. His friend Carl Kiekhaefer asked him to drive a 1951 Chrysler Saratoga in the Carrera Panamericana, the Mexican Road Race. The six-leg race was from the Mexican border in the south to the American border in the north. The first stop was at Oaxaca. At the start, John passed car after car and was gaining on the second-place car when the Chrysler engine quit. So that was that.

Fitch ran the Mexican Road Race again in 1952, this time driving for Mercedes-Benz. The team came in first, second and third. John was fourth in a 300SL.

Off and on during the fifties, John drove for Briggs Cunningham. In 1951, he became the SCCA's first national champion, and in 1953, he and Phil Walters won Sebring and placed third at Le Mans in Cunninghams.

John Fitch's next international race was in 1951. Juan Perón had taken over the government of Argentina. He wanted a Formula One event in Buenos Aires, but the FIA required a preliminary race to test out the course. So a sports car race was organized. A number of Americans were invited, including John Fitch. Without a suitable car, John borrowed a tired Cad-Allard from his friend Tom Cole. The competition was fierce, not only from the Americans but also from Europeans and Argentines, many with faster and better equipment. The 2.2-mile course was on the city streets and, in places, really rough. To make a long story short, Fitch took the checkered flag and was kissed by the race queen, who was also the queen of the country, Evita Perón.

Fitch was in Europe in 1953 where he entered the Monte Carlo Rally, the 1953 Mille Miglia, driving a Nash-Healey whose engine went bad, preventing him from finishing. In June, Fitch drove a Cunningham C3R at Le Mans, where he came in seventh overall and won his class. He drove for John Cooper in a Cooper at the 1953 Grand Prix du Lac at the Aix-les-Bains. He ended up fourth in the Cooper. Fitch drove in the Tourist Trophy and at Reims, and then returned to the United States.

John's greatest year was 1955 when he had become a member of the Mercedes-Benz team, which, led by Juan Fangio and Stirling Moss, won everything. John told

In 1951, John took a friend's J2X Allard to Argentina. He won the race and was kissed by Evita Perón.

me that he thought his greatest drive was the Mille Miglia where he won the GT class in a production 300SL.

Originally, the factory had teamed Fitch at the Mille Miglia with Denis Jenkinson as navigator. During practice, John invented a device, which he made out of wood, to hold a continuous roll of paper with a map of the course. Moss, entered in an SLR, insisted on an all-British crew. At the last minute, Jenks was teamed with Moss. Jenks took the Fitch invention with him and the German mechanics constructed one out of metal. The rest is history. Moss and Jenks won overall.

During that time, John and his family were living in Switzerland. While John was at Monza testing, Rudi Caracciola drove John's pregnant wife, Elizabeth, to the hospital for her to deliver Christopher. Rudi was a great friend and the great prewar Mercedes champion.

In 1956, General Motors honcho Ed Cole asked John to lead a team of Corvettes at Sebring that year. Until then, Corvettes were boulevard cruisers and not selling well. GM was even considering dropping the marque. Three cars were delivered to John at Sebring in mid–February. Race day was March 24. In those few short weeks, John was able to do what Zora Arkus-Duntov considered impossible given the time available.

He turned them into serious competitors that won the production class and the team prize. John led the team and drove at Sebring the following year and at Le Mans in 1960.

When the Corvair came out, it left quite a lot to be desired in terms of handling and performance. John put his not inconsiderable talents to work improving the breed and created the Fitch Sprint. He developed it into a kit that was sold to Chevrolet dealers who did the necessary modifications. The Sprint was so good that it was able to compete in SCCA road races.

John's 18-year racing career is the stuff of much legend, but his most significant contributions are in automotive safety. He designed the course at Lime Rock, among the safest in the world for drivers as well as spectators. Fitch's concern with safety began at Le Mans in 1955 when he was teamed with Pierre Levegh. Before John took a turn at the wheel, Levegh was involved in what many consider to be the most horrendous racing accident ever.

John took great satisfaction for his invention and development of Fitch Inertial Barriers. These ubiquitous barrels that line danger points on our thruways and byways have saved countless lives. Most people assume they are just sand-filled barrels, but

John with his Fitch Sprint Corvair near Lime Rock, Connecticut. Photograph by Larry Berman.

they are much more than that. Without going into the technology, suffice it to say that John was granted a patent.

John and I became acquainted when we worked together during the sixties on advertising projects, he as driver and I as cinematographer. For some years, whenever he was in California, we sailed together on my Newport 30. Since then, we have kept in touch. I was privileged when he asked me to help him with a book about some of his experiences, *Racing with Mercedes*. I discovered, to top off his many other talents, John Fitch was also an excellent writer. His descriptions of fifties-era open-road racing were unparalleled.

In later years, John occupied himself with safety as it relates to racing. When I got involved in a revival event on the streets of Palm Springs in 1985, John was one of the first people I contacted. Since we couldn't afford Fitch Barriers, he advised me to buy large used plastic barrels and fill them with water. They turned out to be very effective and were most kind to cars and drivers. Another of his significant inventions is a movable guardrail. When struck, it moves, thus reducing the impact on car and driver.

In 2007, John was in Los Angeles to attend a Society of Automotive Engineers

John testing his Fitch Inertial Barrier at Lime Rock, Connecticut. Photograph by Larry Berman.

conference held in Hollywood. He and Ken Berg presented a paper, "Are We Flat-Out for Survivable Deceleration? The 1955 Crash at Le Mans—Its Impact on Racing." While John was in Los Angeles, a group of us celebrated his 90th birthday at my home. The following weekend, John was inducted into the Motorsports Hall of Fame. This was a typical Fitch schedule.

For some years, John and I attended the Monterey Historics together. During his trips to California, he always made it a point to include nearby San Jose. Years ago, the first mate of his prewar Caribbean adventure married. Her family, including children and grandchildren live there. He always made it a point to visit his friend's family.

On October 24, 2008, the Petersen Automotive Museum in Los Angeles held a celebration to honor Corvettes as race cars. A large number of Corvette drivers were there, but John was the star. To help celebrate, I put together a book, *Racing with Corvettes: The Early Years*. We had a box of books hot off the press that John and I autographed for his fans.

John at his home in Connecticut in 2010. Photograph by the author.

John was in remarkable good health for most of his life, but in 2011, his physical condition started to fail, and he was hospitalized a number of times. In 2012, John, still living at home, spent much of his time sleeping. A mutual friend and John's neighbor, Don Klein, visited him often. One time Don asked John if he dreamed a lot. John replied that his dreams were wonderful; he would have long and intimate talks with his dear Elizabeth, who had died in 2009. A highlight for John during those last months was when Stirling and Susie Moss came to visit over Labor Day. John Cooper Fitch died peacefully at age 95 on October 31, 2012, at his home in Lakeville, Connecticut, surrounded by his three sons, John, Christopher (Kip) and Stephen.

2

Ed Hugus

Ed Hugus was one of the greats of the fifties and sixties, but an unsung hero. This is undoubtedly due to his quiet and unassuming personality. Although Ed ranked with some of the best of the era, he never beat his own drum.

Ed was one of the very few American winners of the world's premier road racing event, Le Mans, where he competed for ten consecutive years starting in 1956. In 1957, Ed and his co-driver, Count Carel de Beaufort, finished first in class and eighth overall in a Porsche Spyder. After that, when he finished, Ed was always in the top ten overall.

In 1965, Masten Gregory, Jochen Rindt and Ed Hugus were first overall at Le Mans in a Ferrari 275LM entered by Luigi Chinetti's North American Racing Team. Originally, Ed was entered as a relief driver, to take the wheel only if something happened to Gregory or Rindt. During the early hours of the morning, something did happen. Gregory took over while Rindt went off somewhere to sleep. Fog came in and Gregory's glasses got so misted he couldn't see. He came in. But Rindt was nowhere to be found, so Ed took over and drove the rest of the morning hours. After the race ended, Gregory and Rindt were on the podium, but Ed was some distance away. Aided by two gendarmes, he struggled to get through the crowd. However, the ceremony had ended before he arrived. Consequently, some early reports failed to credit Hugus with the win and the misconception has continued to this day.

Edward James Hugus was born on June 30, 1923, at his paternal grandfather's farm in Pennsylvania. His father's family came from Alsace-Lorraine in 1767. Three-quarters of his mother's family came from England; the other quarter was Mohawk Indian. The family moved to Ed's maternal grandfather's farm in Ohio where Ed went to school. When his grandfather died, they returned to Pennsylvania where Ed's father worked in the steel business.

When World War II came along, Ed joined the Army. After basic training at Fort Benning, Georgia, he became a paratrooper with the 11th Airborne Division. In January 1945, after more than a year of combat, the division landed on the island of Luzon in the Philippines. On February 16, the 503rd Parachute Regimental Combat Team made the most spectacular airborne assault of the Pacific war, if not all of World War II: the retaking of Fortress Corregidor, called the Rock.

Top: **Ed Hugus takes the flag at Le Mans in 1956.** *Bottom:* **Hugus in a Ferrari 250GT at Le Mans in 1962. Both photographs: Ed Hugus collection.**

C-47 aircraft, circling in train, each carrying 27 troopers, had to make three passes at under 600 feet to drop three "sticks" of troopers on a patch 250 yards long and 100 yards wide, while flying into a 20-mile-an-hour headwind and enduring intense small-arms fire. The drop zone was a small plateau that is on top of the five-square-mile polliwog-shaped island. The jump master attempted to time the jump to compensate for the wind, but even so, some troops were blown over the cliffs or landed among the enemy. Some men were killed by enemy fire while still aboard the aircraft. Others were impaled by rebar in broken concrete or splintered trees in the drop zone. The 503rd dropped two battalions, one at 8 AM, the other at noon and a third on February 17. All in all, they killed 6,600 Japanese soldiers and secured the island after ten days of fighting. Ed Hugus was 21 years old.

The recapture of Corregidor Island was the crowning achievement of the Philip-

2. Ed Hugus

Ed and Peter Jopp drove a Cobra (4) at Le Mans in 1963. Their engine failed while they were running in tenth place. Ed Hugus collection.

pine campaign. Of this drop, Ed remarked, "I was one of the few who survived. Not many of us did." After the war was won, he served with the occupation in Japan.

Mustered out in 1946, Ed returned to Pennsylvania and got a job building coke ovens. In 1949, he discovered sports cars and got a few dollars together to buy an MGTC. The next year, he and a partner started an MG dealership in Pittsburgh. Soon afterwards, they added Jaguar to their lineup.

He joined the SCCA in 1951 and ran his first race at MacDill Air Force Base in a Jaguar XK120. The record shows that Ed continued to compete through 1969. He finished 56 races and won 8. He drove a large variety of cars, Ferrari being the most at 30 times. He was in Cuba in 1958 when Juan Fangio was kidnapped, and the race was red flagged because of numerous wrecks and injuries. By then, Hugus and Carroll Shelby had become good friends. Shelby is credited with a third in that race.

Ed drove an Alfa Giulietta Spyder at the very first race at the then new Virginia International Raceway in 1955. Two others drove Alfas on that same occasion: Carroll Shelby and Bob Grossman. All three finished nose to tail, with Shelby taking the checkered flag.

Ed's best finish at Sebring was in 1960 when he and Augie Pabst drove a North American Racing Team 250GT to first in class and fourth overall. He raced at Sebring a total of 15 times. The two drove another NART 250GT at Le Mans that year to seventh

Ed (wearing dark glasses) entered his own 550 RS Porsche and drove it, with Count Carel de Beaufort, to win eighth overall and first in class at Le Mans in 1957. Ed Hugus collection.

overall and second in class. Augie remembers Ed with a great deal of affection and respect, remarking, "Ed was a real gentleman. I never heard him say an unkind word about anyone." Ed's favorite expression was "I don't have a dog in that fight."

Ed told me that the most important thing for him about racing was that it was a lot of fun. He didn't let it dominate his life because he was involved with other things. Duane Carter offered him a chance to test at Indy in 1958 but he simply couldn't take the time to do it. Actually, he was given several opportunities to become a professional race driver, but business commitments, investors and family came first. Insofar as racing was concerned, Ed was the consummate amateur.

Eventually, Ed ended up with three different car dealerships in Pittsburgh. He was the U.S. distributor of Isis Formula Juniors that were made by Alejandro De Tomaso in Italy.

Shortly after Carroll Shelby started to produce Cobras, Ed became the first dealer and then took on the eastern states distributorship. After Cobras became a sensational success, the Ford Motor Company tried to take the distributorship away from Shelby by making Cobras and selling directly to distributors and dealers. Shelby called Ed and told him about it. Ed, true friend that he was, replied, "No problem; don't worry about

Ed in a 250 GT Ferrari (20) at Sebring in 1960. Phil Hill is in the 56 car. Ed Hugus collection.

it." Partly because of Ed's loyalty and intervention with Ford, Shelby was able to keep the project. He and Ed remained close friends through the years.

In 1963, Ed entered his Cobra in the 24 Hours of Le Mans, at a not inconsiderable expense. It was the first Cobra to race at Le Mans. While he and his co-driver, Peter Jopp, failed to finish, they were credited with 23rd place.

In 1968, Ed sold all of his Pittsburgh businesses and moved to Jacksonville, Florida, where he took on the Southeast distributorship for BMW. His last drive was in a BMW 2002 at Sebring in 1969. In 1974, BMW wanted the distributorship back, so he sold it and retired.

I met Ed in January of 1992 on the occasion of Briggs Cunningham's 85th birthday party. Somehow, we seemed to click and remained good friends. Ed and my son, David, became especially close and, even up to a few days before Ed died, they talked on the phone frequently. Ed took him under his wing, so to speak, and advised David on all sorts of business and personal matters. David told me that Ed said on one phone call, "If you don't learn something new every day, then you're not paying attention." David said he tried to live by those words. We always got together at the Monterey Historics as Ed lived in Pebble Beach.

Ed met his wife, Barbara, on the island of St. Thomas in 1972. According to Barbara, a physician, "I was on a mini-sabbatical from Massachusetts General Hospital and the Harvard Medical School where I was a professor and department chair. Ed was vacationing there too, and we maintained a close relationship through the years. But we didn't marry until 1992, when I retired." By then, Ed's only family was a distant niece, so he acquired Barbara's. She said, "He had known my four children since they were teenagers and had a close relationship with all of them. And Ed adored my grandchildren."

Edward James Hugus died on June 29, 2006, one day before his 83rd birthday.

He was a member of the Greatest Generation, which won World War II and went on to help develop the United States into the world power that it is today. He was also an important player in the development of U.S. road racing during the second half of the 20th century.

Ed at his home in Pebble Beach in 1996. Photograph by the author.

3

Paul Newman

How can starring in a movie change an actor's life? Not just change, but set it on a new and different course? The actor was Paul Newman and the movie was *Winning*, which came out in 1969. The film is about a professional race car driver—played by Newman—who married a single mother, played by Paul's wife, Joanne Woodward.

When the movie came out, Paul Newman was already a big star. He started his acting career on Broadway, and his first movie was *The Silver Chalice* in 1954. He starred with Elizabeth Taylor in *Cat on a Hot Tin Roof* (1958). That same year he appeared with Frank Sinatra and Eva Marie Saint in a live TV version of Thornton Wilder's play *Our Town*. Other hits such as *Exodus*, *Hud*, *Cool Hand Luke* and *Butch Cassidy and the Sundance Kid* followed. Paul won the Academy Award for *The Color of Money* plus three Golden Globes and an Emmy. He also directed five feature films, including four starring Joanne Woodward.

Paul Newman led a most extraordinary life. Not only was he a movie and television actor; he was a film director and producer, amateur and professional race car driver, race team owner, innovative entrepreneur, political activist, and generous philanthropist.

Although *Winning* is about oval-track racing, Newman became enthralled with road racing. As Steve Parker wrote in his obituary, "He was not a wealthy dilettante who spent weekends slumming with gear-heads and wrenches; he was a skilled, serious, professional and world-class race driver as well as one of the most successful team owners in the sport's history. Had he never acted, his racing career alone would have garnered him great fame and fortune."

Paul Leonard Newman was born on January 26, 1925, in Shaker Heights, Ohio, near Cleveland. Paul's father was Jewish and his mother Catholic. Nevertheless, he always claimed to be Jewish. Newman was interested in acting at a young age. His first part was as the court jester in a grade-school production of *Robin Hood*.

After graduating from Shaker Heights High School in 1943, he went to Ohio University where he tried to join the Navy V-12 pilot-training program. He wanted to be a pilot. But when the Navy discovered Paul was color blind, he was sent to boot camp and then trained as a radioman, bombardier and gunner for torpedo bombers. In 1944,

Paul was sent to the Naval Air Station at Barbers Point on Oahu, Hawaii. (It was also called John Rogers Field which was closed in the nineties and later reopened as Kalaeloa Airport.) At Barbers Point he flew in torpedo bomber squadrons that trained pilots.

The Navy's torpedo bomber was the Grumman TBF Avenger that became operational in the latter half of 1942. It had a crew of three, the pilot, rear turret gunner and a radio operator–bombardier with a ventrally mounted .30-caliber machine gun located behind the bomb bay. The TBF had a silhouette similar to the F4F Wildcat. During the battle for Guadalcanal the famous Japanese ace Saburo Sakai thought he was sneaking up under the tail of a Wildcat, only to be seriously wounded by the radioman-gunner of a TBF.

Next, Newman was stationed on an aircraft carrier in the Pacific, the USS *Bunker Hill*. During the assault on Okinawa, the ship was hit by two kamikaze suicide planes and sank, suffering the second-worst causalities of the battle: 393 killed, 600 wounded. But before the attack, Paul's pilot had developed an ear infection and, along with Paul, was sent ashore for treatment.

Paul Newman was in the U.S. Navy from 1943 to 1946. He served in the Pacific Theatre. Paul Newman collection.

After mustering out in 1946, Newman returned to complete his bachelor's degree in 1949 at Kenyon College in Gambier, Ohio. Paul earned a Bachelor of Arts in drama and also one in economics. He also achieved an advanced degree in drama at Yale in 1954 and studied under Lee Strasberg at the Actors' Studio in New York City.

The thing that got him into racing was training for the film *Winning*. He said, "[It was] the first thing that I ever found I had any grace in." He told *Vintage Racecar* editor Casey Annis, "I have no physical abilities. I was a terrible skier, a terrible football player, a terrible tennis player and a terrible dancer." Aside from acting, racing turned out to be something he could do and do well. He trained at the Watkins Glen Racing School to prepare for his starring role in *Winning*. In addition, Bob Bondurant, technical director of *Winning*, spent many months with Paul at Bob's school and at various tracks training Paul. As a consequence, he entered his own Saab 96 in a Trans-American Sedan race at Virginia International Raceway on July 31, 1966. He managed a 16th overall.

Shortly after finishing the film, Newman joined the SCCA, acquired a Lotus Elan, took driver training and got an SCCA license. Paul's wife, Joanne, wasn't exactly ecstatic over Paul's new hobby and neither were those who employed him in the movie business.

In addition to the potential for not being able to work because of injury, the problem was insurance. It is sometimes difficult to insure an actor who spends his weekends on race tracks. But by then Paul was such a big star that he could get away with it. Nevertheless, he would sometimes enter under a pseudonym.

His first win was at Thompson, CT. He went on to win four SCCA National Championships. Driving a 280Z Datsun in 1976, he won the D-Production category. Then in 1979 he won C-Production and in 1986 and 1987 he won GT-1.

Newman drove not only as an amateur but also as a professional. He was 47 years old when he started to drive Datsuns (later Nissans) for the Bob Sharp Racing team in the Trans-Am Series. He also drove for Dick Barber Racing in a Porsche, finishing second overall and winning his class at Le Mans in 1979. He even tried the Baja 1000 in

Paul Newman starred in the film *Winning* (1969). Paul Newman collection.

2004. He celebrated his 70th birthday on February 4, 2005, driving in the 24 Hours of Daytona. He is in the Guinness Book of World Records as the oldest driver to win a professionally sanctioned race after winning the 1995 Daytona.

The record indicates that Paul Newman drove in a total of 108 races. He won 3 overall and his class twice. He was second overall in 6 and 5 times third. Paul sat on the pole 4 times and stood on the podium 14 times.

Paul's involvement in racing extended beyond driving. He was also an owner of professional teams. For a short time, he owned a Can-Am team and he was a partner in the Formula Atlantic team Newman-Wachs Racing. In addition, he owned a

NASCAR Winston Cup car he later sold to Roger Penske.

His most notable and successful time, however, was when he and Carl Haas formed the Newman-Haas team in 1983 for the CART (Championship Auto Racing Teams) series. Two World Champions—Nigel Mansell and Mario Andretti—drove for them. Newman's celebrity as an actor also attracted some of the sport's best sponsors, including Texaco and McDonald's. Since its beginning, the team has achieved more than 100 victories as well as series championships in 1993, 2002 and 2004–2007. Andretti remarked, "Paul was a real asset. Many thought he was only superficially involved, but it's the exact opposite. He was in with both feet."

On Paul's death, Carl Haas noted, "Paul and I have been partners for 26 years and I have come to know his passion, humor and above all, his generosity." Mario Andretti said, "He was a friend for many years. We first met in 1967. When Newman-Haas was founded, I guess I was one of the architects. I spent 12 years of my career driving for him and Carl until I retired." Competitors also appreciated Newman. Bobby Rahal observed, "He was a man of great courage, determination and integrity. His generosity knew no bounds."

Newman was a talented cook. He made his own special salad dressing that was so good it developed into a

Top: **Paul Newman married Joanne Woodward in Las Vegas in 1958. Paul Newman collection.** *Bottom:* **In 1995 Paul Newman won the 24 Hours of Daytona. He was 70 years old. Paul Newman collection.**

Paul Newman (left) and Carl Haas formed the Newman/Haas Racing Team that had a host of victories. Paul Newman collection.

company and brand, Newman's Own, in 1982. Offerings soon expanded to include pasta sauce, lemonade, popcorn, salsa, wine and other products. All profits go to charity. By the end of 2005, more than $250 million had been donated.

One of the Newman family charities is the Hole in the Wall Gang Camp. This started in 1988 as a summer camp for seriously sick children located in Ashford, Connecticut. The organization has expanded to include additional camps in other parts of the United States as well as in Ireland, France and Israel. More than 12,000 children participate every year free of charge. Newman's generosity didn't stop there. Quite a number of other charities were associated with and supported by Newman.

Paul was married two times, the first to Jackie Witte in 1949. Paul and Jackie had a son, Scott, and two daughters, Susan and Stephanie. After Scott died in 1978 from a drug overdose, Paul started the Scott Newman Center for drug abuse prevention. After his divorce, Newman married actress Joanne Woodward in 1958. They had three daughters: Elinor Teresa, Melissa and Claire. The Newmans were never part of the Hollywood scene but lived quietly in Westport, Connecticut. On May 25, 2007, Paul announced he was retiring from acting.

During the eighties, I attempted to organize a series for older and retired champions. Fortunately, or not, it never really materialized. Nevertheless, Paul was one of the first drivers on board and was always very supportive of my efforts. We talked frequently on the phone.

In June 2008, it was reported in the press that Paul Newman, a former chain smoker, was diagnosed with terminal lung cancer. On August 13, 2008, Lime Rock Park was closed for an hour and a half to honor Paul Newman. Accompanied by his family, close friends, Skip Barber and mechanics on his race teams, Paul toured the track in his Corvette. He had come to say goodbye. He died on September 26 at age 83 in his home surrounded by family.

4

Mary Davis

Mary Davis was an extraordinary woman. After serving in the Marine Corps, she went on to an astoundingly successful career in business. Not only that, she was a championship race car driver. While driving, she was well known for her long blonde hair streaming out from under her helmet.

Mary Davis was born on June 10, 1928, in San Diego. Her parents were of pioneer stock from Texas and Virginia. In 1943 at age 15, she dropped out of Fremont High School in Los Angeles and joined the Marine Corps Women's Reserve (commonly called BAMS) and served on active duty during World War II. Asked why she joined the Marines, she replied, "I thought they had the cutest uniforms." She told me, "After joining, I spent the next year repairing diesel engine fuel injectors on M4 tanks at a Marine Corps Base near Isthmus Creek not far from San Francisco. A year before the war ended, somehow the government found out about my age and I was honorably discharged."

Mary said, "After my discharge, I went to visit a friend in San Francisco. There was this fellow named Bob Drake operating the switchboard in my hotel. We started going out and ended up in Reno two weeks later getting married. We stayed together through thick and mostly thin for the next 18 years."

Mary and Bob moved to Southern California, and Mary went to the Lumbleau School of Real Estate. She got her license and worked selling Hollywood and Beverly Hills property, making considerable commissions. Bob pursued his now-and-then profession of deep-sea diving.

One day, the two drove to Monterey to see a race at Pebble Beach. As Mary told it, "I immediately had a tremendous urge to participate in road racing, so I bought an MG." Soon, she entered several time trials. Her first race was at the Santa Barbara Airport on the weekend of September 5–6, 1953. It was also the first race at that venue and was organized by the California Sports Car Club (not then part of the SCCA). Mary entered her MG in the Ladies' Race and won her first time out. During the fifties, Mary was at or near the front in every ladies' race in which she participated. Often, she drove for wealthy sportsman Joe Lubin in the same cars Bob Drake raced in the main event. Her collection of trophies numbered more than 30. She raced through

Mary's Marine group in 1943. Mary is second from left. Mary Davis collection.

(From left) Bob Drake, Mary and Joe Lubin at Santa Barbara in 1958. Mary Davis collection.

4. Mary Davis

Mary in a Cooper (49) and Jack McAfee (88) in a Ferrari at the Del Mar suburb of San Diego in 1959.

1959; her record shows that she entered 29 races, won 5 of them overall and won her class 12 times.

Since Mary was qualified driver-wise and also photogenic, she was asked to participate in the 1957 Mobilgas Economy Run, a cross-country driving competition featuring the top economy cars along a set route. It turned out to be one of the most hectic times in her life. Since all entries were required to have a navigator, Mary asked fellow lady race driver Ginny Sims to join her. First of all, there was practice. There were times when the two practiced for 18 hours! But practice was not like the actual race. Mary remembered, "In the actual Run, being 10 seconds late will disqualify you. It is much harder than road racing. It's the most harrowing, nerve-racking experience I've ever been through with no speed involved." Driving a Plymouth, she and Ginny ended up winning overall their first time out. They competed against three former winners. She also defeated Betty Skelton, who held more records than any other woman driver.

Mary's first business venture was to open a restaurant in Los Angeles. She told me the story:

> Bob and I decided we wanted to open our own restaurant, so we looked for a location. We wanted something on Sunset Boulevard near where the then popular series *77 Sunset Strip* was filmed. But nothing suitable was available. Finally, we found a closed restaurant on Beverly Boulevard. The only problem was that I was the only one who had any money. Since Bob and I were married at the time, I guess he thought my money was his money.

Mary won the Ladies' Race at Santa Barbara in 1957. Mary Davis collection.

They bought the restaurant business and took over the lease on the building. The Grand Prix opened on Valentine's Day 1957 at 8204 Beverly Boulevard. Mary worked all day every day, while Bob only showed up to count the take. Everyone who was anyone in Southern California sports car racing could be found there at one time or another. Mary was the person who actually ran the Grand Prix. "At first," she said, "I thought Bob would actually work there, but he never really wanted to work very much at anything."

I wrote in the *Sports Car Journal* magazine at the time, "The restaurant is a true sports car enthusiast's delight with magnificent murals of famous European races adorning the walls and sports car racing films shown every Thursday night." Eventually she and Bob came to a parting of the ways. By 1961, she said, "I was finally fed up and wanted out of the marriage and the restaurant too." She gave the Grand Prix to Bob in the divorce settlement. He sold it soon thereafter, and the new owners transformed it into a gay bar.

Advertisement for the Grand Prix restaurant, 1957. Mary Davis collection.

While the Grand Prix was a success, two years later an even greater challenge and opportunity presented itself. The City of Redondo Beach was developing its yacht harbor. Mary knew that this would be an ideal location for a fuel dock on the Redondo Beach waterfront, so she put in a bid to the city. Instead, she was forced by the city to bid on the entire eight-acre parcel. So Mary envisioned an upscale hotel and restaurant complex. In 1960, she borrowed $8,000 to bid on the parcel. The bid was accepted, and she borrowed another $1,800,000 and built the famous Portofino Inn. She started the project with a contractor (who also entered cars in sports car races), but because of labor problems he bowed out. Mary became her own general contractor.

The complex included a hotel, two restaurants, and two bars, about one-fourth of the yacht harbor slips, some offices, an apartment building and the fuel dock. The marina opened in 1962, the apartment building in 1964 and the rest in 1965. The Portofino became a landmark and another racer hangout. It was the end point for the famous Brock Yates Cannonball Run, an unauthorized race from New York to California that took place in 1971, 1972, 1975 and 1979. The winner had to travel the distance in the fastest possible time. It inspired three films, including the Burt Reynolds 1981 comedy classic *The Cannonball Run*. The Portofino was also the end point for the One Lap of America event.

Mary lived in one of the apartments and ran the whole kit and caboodle with a wise and even hand. I moved into a second-floor apartment there in 1965. I always said I lived below Mary Davis, as her apartment was directly above mine. I was a double tenant because I also rented a slip there for my sailboat. Vasek Polak maintained an apartment, as did Danny Ongais. Mario Andretti and the Unser brothers were frequent hotel guests as well as many other luminaries of the sport.

During her time in Redondo Beach, Mary served as the president of the chamber of commerce, was an elected member of the South Bay Hospital District and was seriously proposed for mayor, an honor she eventually decided to forgo.

In 1986, Mary sold the Portofino. With some of the money, she started her own

Mary Davis and Carroll Shelby at a 2001 gathering in Woodland Hills, California. Mary Davis collection.

Top: **Mary (right) with her best friend, Ginny Sims, on Mary's yacht, 1986. Ginny Simms collection.** *Right:* **Mary at her home in Palm Springs in 1987. Photograph by the author.**

bank in Redondo Beach, the Bay Cities National Bank, where I still have my account. A few years ago, the bank was merged with another and Mary retired again with more well-earned gains. She had not achieved her lifelong dream of becoming the world's richest woman. But as a multi-millionaire when she died, she might have come close.

After selling the Portofino, Mary married her longtime companion, who had been her hotel manager. She acquired an oceangoing yacht and they looked forward to a fun-filled retirement. Unfortunately, her new husband, a heavy smoker, died from lung cancer about a year later. She had spent an entire year caring for him. I remarked to her that I hoped the next time she would choose a non-smoker for a boyfriend.

Mary had no children. Her family consisted of many nieces and nephews. In retirement, she bought a home in La Quinta (near Palm Springs) and one on Coronado Island near San Diego.

Mary died at age 86 on December 8, 2014. "She was just a fantastic person," said her nephew, Tom Preston. She was good to everyone, just a sweetheart, I loved her dearly." Preston cared for her during her four-year illness.

On January 11, 2015, her many friends had a gathering to remember her at the Portofino. Some of us there voiced words of remembrance.

5

Bill Devin

In the July 1961 edition of *Car and Driver* magazine, Henry Manney described Bill Devin as "the Enzo Ferrari of Okie Flats." Although William Elbert Devin was born in Rocky, Oklahoma, on November 13, 1915, almost all of his racing and automotive activities were in Southern California.

In the early fifties, Bill raced, but he is best known for designing and building sports cars. He did build his first car in Oklahoma, however, for his younger brother, Gene. It used a washing machine motor; its suspension was old valve springs and he made the body from a metal sign.

Bill's dad had a Chevrolet agency and garage in Rocky. Young Bill learned to weld, and he worked on oil drilling rigs. But as Henry Manney said, "Oklahoma blew away, business blew away and the Devin family followed the trail to California." It was the late thirties and Devin went to work at Douglas Aircraft, where he was employed to build and maintain jigs and fixtures used to manufacture aircraft. Next, he was the crew chief on the flight line for the Douglas A-20 Havoc light bomber. World War II came along, and Bill joined the Navy. He was assigned as a machinist's mate working on landing craft. Then he was posted to an assault transport unit where he maintained landing craft.

After spending two and a half years in the Navy, Bill was mustering out when the war ended. Bill went to live in Montour, Iowa, near his wife's home, where he opened Chrysler-Plymouth and Crosley dealerships, plus a farm implement business.

In 1950, he sold out and moved to California. He bought the Chrysler-Plymouth agency in Fontana. After attending a sports car race in Santa Ana, he got interested in racing himself. Bill bought a Crosley Hot Shot and modified it to get more power from the small CIBA 45.8 engine. He entered the Hot Shot in the novice race at Buchanan Field in August 1951 and won. Next there was a 100-mile race where he was the class winner. He raced the Crosley four more times and won his class every time. Enamored with racing and sports cars, Bill sold his agency and formed a partnership with Ernie McAfee to import and sell Siatas. They bought 25 Siatas, but were unable to retail them, so they sold all the cars to another company and dissolved the partnership.

Bill became interested in Ferraris and bought a 2.6-liter 212 and started to race it.

He owned and raced a number of different Ferrari models. He raced five times, scoring three overall thirds.

Then he bought a Deutsch-Bonnet (DB) with a Panhard engine. Not satisfied with its performance, he built a special based on the DB and the Panhard engine with a Devin-designed fiberglass body. Bill built 11 more Devin-Panhards in 1955. He and Jim Orr entered a few races. Orr himself went on to win the SCCA National (Class H) Championship in the Devin-Panhard.

Bill gave up racing and formed Devin Enterprises in 1956 to manufacture fiberglass bodies. At that time, Devin Enterprises was in El Monte, California. Bill was making fiberglass bodies by the hundreds. The idea was to replace the stock body on whatever car you had. There were a few others in the same business, but Bill's products were unique. His were not only the most beautiful, but he also made them in 27 different sizes to fit almost any chassis. Each body came in two pieces with one half fitting inside the other, creating an economic shipping package. Additionally, the seats were an integral part and the deck lids were finished off complete with hinges. Bill took great care

The Devin factory floor in El Monte in 1958. Bill Devin collection.

and pride in his molds. The result was a body of the highest quality. The complete body cost only $295, and they were sold all over the world.

I first came into contact with Bill because of my association with OCee Ritch. (OCee is not a typo; it's an American Indian name.) In 1956, both of us were into auto-related advertising and public relations. With the idea that the whole might be greater than the parts, we formed a partnership. One of OCee's clients was Devin Enterprises.

By 1956, the aftermarket fiberglass-body business was going great guns. The Devin body had become the undisputed leader in the field. Bill's appetite for building complete cars had been whetted with the Devin-Panhard. Serendipitously, a fellow in Northern Ireland, Malcolm MacGregor, had designed a rolling chassis somewhat like a Lister. Malcolm was looking for a body and came across one of the Devin ads OCee and I had placed. He got in touch with Bill, and—to make a long story short—the Devin SS was born. The resultant car was truly outstanding. With a curb weight 1,000 pounds less than a Corvette, but with the same power, performance was stupendous. OCee and I fell in love with it and, of course, were excited by the prospect of promoting such a product.

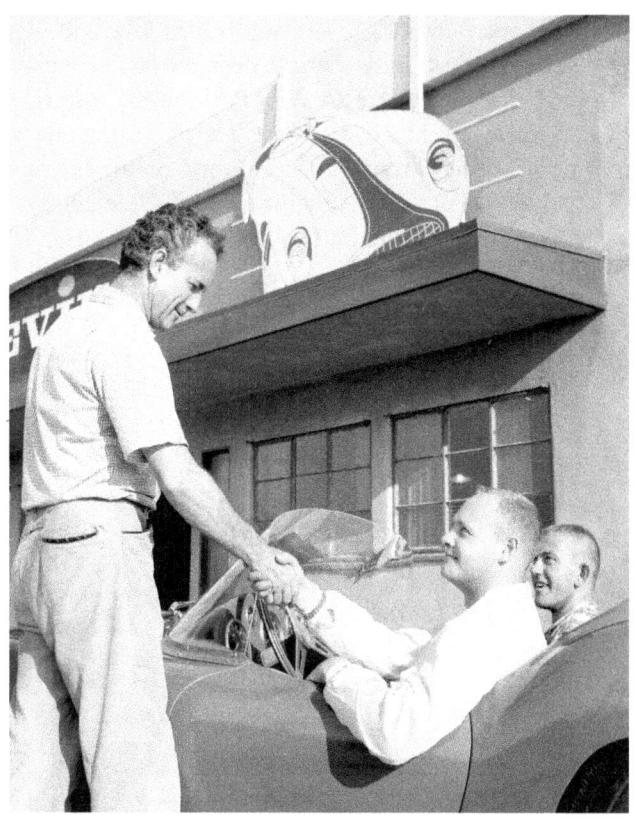

Bill Devin delivering the first Devin SS to Art Evans (driving) and his brother Robb in 1958. Art Evans collection.

MacGregor and Devin made an agreement whereby MacGregor would build rollers in Northern Ireland and ship them to California where Bill would install Corvette running gear and Devin bodies. Bill had designed a new and even more beautiful body for the car. The problem was that MacGregor demanded payment before shipment. After the first chassis, Bill didn't have sufficient cash. With hat in hand, I persuaded my father to finance the operation and we created a new company called Evans Industries. The plan was for Evans to pay MacGregor, Devin to complete each unit and Evans to do the marketing.

Bill completed the first car in 1958, and it became our demonstrator. Our costs required that we set the retail price at about the same cost as a 300SL but significantly more than for an XK140. To put it mildly, and in spite of some great publicity, sales were not brisk. Bill set out to design a less expensive sports car. He built a chassis and body designed around VW or Porsche 356 running gear, which I christened the Devin D (for Deutschland). When Chevrolet came out with the Corvair the next year, Bill modified the D frame to accept the Corvair engine and transmission and—voila!—we had the Devin C. Eventually, we sold some 200 Ds and Cs. About half were complete cars while the other half were delivered as kits.

Advertisement for Evans Industries in racing programs. Bill Devin collection.

During that time, we were truly a jolly band and had a lot of fun. Bob Bondurant joined us as parts manager with my brother, Robb, his helper. Pete Woods was hired to be our sales manager. OCee and I had personally bought the prototype from Malcolm, and I raced it during 1959. I made a deal with my buddy Andy Porterfield, who was then working and racing a Corvette for an LA Chevrolet dealer. We put a hot Vette engine in our car, and Andy raced it at the first Times Grand Prix. Unfortunately, he failed to finish because of a mechanical problem, but our driver in the Ladies' Race, Ginny Sims, set a speed record of 163 mph down the back straight at Riverside.

To be blunt, Bill was never the easiest person with whom to deal. While undoubtedly a brilliant designer, he sometimes tended to be stubborn and opinionated. And I guess I wasn't always that easy to get along with either. In retrospect, it's obvious that neither of us were very good at running the business part of the operation. We made a lot of mistakes and, while the products were outstanding, eventually everything came apart.

At my end, my father had a heart attack and had to retire. OCee and I lost our major client and the partnership went broke. Bill soldiered on for a few years and eventually tried to go into the roof-rack manufacturing business. Fortunately for Bill, his wife Middie had gone into real estate and did very well at it.

When they lived in Yucaipa, Bill had a large garage next to the home where he had an office and shop. Until his death, he provided advice and parts for those who

5. Bill Devin

(From left) Ken Miles, Art Evans, Sr., and Bill Devin at a party at Evans Industries in Pasadena. Bill Devin collection.

Bill in 1979. Photograph by the author.

owned his cars. I would visit them often and we would chew over old times.

In 1985, I was able to buy an SS I found in the proverbial farmer's barn. Also, I traded an extra car I had for a C. I had begun running them in a few vintage races, but always with Bill listed as the entrant. He enjoyed going to Laguna Seca for the Monterey Historics in his large motorhome and camping near the circuit. Bill would always sit in my paddock and enjoy the camaraderie that developed among Devin vintage drivers and their families. Bill was always the center of attention. Andy Porterfield would race an SS in remembrance of his time at Riverside.

My fondest remembrance of Bill was in November 1990 when we celebrated his 75th birthday with a grand gathering at my Palm Springs home. A large number of friends came to

Devin cars were celebrated at the 1998 Monterey Historics. Bill Devin collection.

pay their respects. Phil Hill, Carroll Shelby, Zora Arkus-Duntov, John Von Neumann, Vasek Polak and Dan Gurney were a few of the guests I can recall. Bill was pleased so many had come to honor him and was as happy as I had seen him in a long time.

In 2000, Bill became ill and Middie had to take him to the hospital. When I visited him there, he was 85 years old. He told me that this was the only time he had been a patient and it was also the first time he had ever seen a doctor! A few days later, he was gone. Bill died on November 24, 2000. Middie asked me to deliver the eulogy. On that occasion, I said, "For me, knowing Bill and having the honor of being in business with him and racing his cars has been a real adventure. Thank you, Bill. Farewell, good friend. Godspeed."

Bill was survived by his wife, Mildred (Middie) Delia Devin, sons William Devin III, Joel Devin and John Devin, plus daughters Valerie Provines and Linda Ryssman. Middie died on February 15, 2003. She was 89.

Today, one of my treasures is my Devin D. It is the prototype (VIN DD-P) that Bill gave me on one of my birthdays. My aging memory doesn't remember which one. Today, Bill's cars are valuable collector items and much-desired by those who compete in vintage events and concours d'elegance.

6

Jay Chamberlain

Jay Chamberlain was one of those Americans who started racing during the fifties in Southern California and then, because they were so successful, were invited to go to Europe and race in the big time. Jay drove both Formula One and sports cars for Colin Chapman's Team Lotus and became a distributor of Lotus cars during the late fifties and early sixties. His best finish was at Le Mans in 1957 when he and Herbert MacKay-Fraser won their class in a Lotus.

Jay Clifford Chamberlain was born on December 29, 1925, in Los Angeles. He grew up in the San Fernando Valley and attended North Hollywood High School. But rather than devote himself to his studies, he was more interested in cars. Like some others in Southern California during that time, he was enthusiastic about hot rods. Jay built his own rod that he raced on the streets and competed on the dry lakes.

Jay joined the Navy in 1943 and was sent to Farragut, Idaho, for boot camp. Having grown up in Southern California, the frigid weather in Idaho was a chilling experience.

Out of boot camp he was sent to the South Pacific and is listed on the crew roster of the USS *Nicholas*. The ship was DD-449, a Fletcher-class destroyer named after the first commandant of Marines, a hero of the Revolutionary War. She was the flagship of Destroyer Squadron 21. Commissioned on June 4, 1942, she participated in major battles from Guadalcanal through the Philippines to the Japanese surrender in Tokyo Bay. The most dramatic action took place in Manila Bay on February 16, 1945.

The assault on Corregidor, the Rock, with its many caves, included an airborne drop on "topside," the small plateau topping the island. Simultaneously, an Army amphibian force was to land on a small beach. The softening-up process included heavy bombers unloading on the island while the *Nicholas* ran dangerously close in to lob its five-inch shells into the many caves hiding big guns and to expose gun positions by drawing fire. While this action was taking place, a long line of mine sweepers was clearing the bay of mines to enable the amphibious assault.

A Marine gunnery unit on a mine sweeper needed a 20 mm cannon expert and Jay, a gunner's mate, was detached and sent to help the Marines. When a sweeper's cable cut a mine loose, it floated to the surface and was exploded with gunfire.

The spectacular view of the bay and the deeds of the greatest generation on that day are the essence of our history: the airmen dropping bombs, the Marines exploding mines, and the *Nicholas* at flank speed paralleling the coast firing at the cliffs. Then a long line of C-47s lumbered in and circled, making multiple passes dropping multi-colored parachutes, while Army landing craft cut long white wakes on the blue sea as they approached the beach. The topside of Corregidor became festooned with multi-colored parachute silk while PT boats darted inshore to pick up paratroopers who had drifted into the water.

We suffered 900 casualties with 207 killed, as we liberated the island from the Japanese, who lost 6,600 men in the Battle for Corregidor. We gave the Philippines their independence as a free nation on July 4, 1946.

The topside assault was made by the 503rd Parachute Regimental Combat Team. While Jay was popping off mines out in the bay, Ed Hugus of Chapter 2 was dropping onto the Rock! Jay was honorably discharged in 1945.

Back home, Jay took advantage of the government's guarantee to veterans of 52 weeks of unemployment benefits at $20 a week. Living off that $20, Jay took up where he had left off, driving hot rods, often in illegal drag races on public streets. Next, he graduated to racing Midgets and Sprint cars on local oval dirt tracks while working as a garage mechanic.

One of the hot rods Jay built was the famous Eliminator. It was a 1927 Model T Ford roadster fitted with a flathead V8 engine and Bendix aircraft brakes. He ran it in California Roadster Association oval-track races. It was later acquired by Frank "Duffy" Livingstone, the father of go-karts, who drove it in many sports-car road races. In 1953, *Hot Rod* magazine featured it in an article titled "How to Build a Sports Car." When Duffy and I were racing at Paramount Ranch on March 10, 1957, he told me that he had bought the car from Jay in 1954. Duffy won the Consolation Race that day at Paramount and I took his picture. In 2003, the Eliminator was sold at auction for $93,500.

Jay's first wife, Beverly, suggested that he take advantage of the sports car craze and go into business. So Jay opened a small repair shop in Burbank, California, that he named Jay Chamberlain Imported Cars. He started to race his stock Jaguar Mark V, a four-door sedan. His first big-time race was on May 5, 1950, in the first Carrera Panamericana (the Mexican Road Race). According to Jay's son, Jaime,

Jay in his Navy uniform, 1944. Jay Chamberlain collection courtesy of his son, Jaime.

My dad and his navigator and friend, Jorgen Thayssen, drove in the first Carrera Panamericana in my dad's Jaguar Mark V. Unfortunately, a broken piston caused their retirement from the multi-day timed event. The race started in Ciudad Juarez and finished 2,106 miles later in Ciudad Cuauhtemoc, on the Guatemalan border. There were 123 cars entered for this race, mostly from Mexico and the U.S.A.

The first time Jay drove in a sports car race was at Torrey Pines on November 27, 1954. He was the co-driver with Ignacio Lozano, who was the editor and publisher of *La Opinion*, the Los Angeles Spanish-language newspaper. In 1974, President Ford appointed Lozano the U.S. ambassador to El Salvador, where he served until President Carter was elected. The Torrey Pines course was laid out on streets of an abandoned World War II Army base just north of San Diego. They had entered Jay's Jaguar Special in the Six-Hour race but failed to finish because of a broken water hose.

One day a customer—George Buchanan—came to Jay's shop and asked Jay to prepare his Lotus Mark IV for racing. Jay was very impressed with the car. He was delighted when George asked him to co-drive in the Six-Hour race at Torrey Pines on October 22, 1955. They finished 28th overall and second in Class G. On January 14, 1956, Jay, again with Lozano, drove a D-Type Jaguar in the third Torrey Pines Six-Hour race for Hollywood Jaguar dealer Charles Hornburg. Mechanical problems prevented them from finishing. (That 1956 weekend was the last race ever held at Torrey Pines. Torrey Pines is still there, but now it's a golf course.)

Jay drove in Formula One for Colin Chapman. This photograph was taken in England in 1962. Jay Chamberlain collection courtesy of his son, Jaime.

On April 17, 1955, Jay entered Pebble Beach and drove the Jaguar Special he had built. He finished but not among the front runners. His buddy Nacho Lozano did better, winning the Cypress Point Handicap in his stock Jaguar. A few weeks later, Jay ran his Jaguar Special at Bakersfield, where he managed a not very creditable 37th overall in the main event.

While attending the 12 Hours of Sebring in 1956, Jay ran into Lotus honcho Colin Chapman. Jay told Chapman about the 1956 race at Torrey Pines. Chapman told Jay about a dual-purpose sports car he was planning (the Lotus Elite). The end result of that meeting was that Jay became a Lotus dealer and eventually the U.S. Lotus distributor.

I remember that I met Jay at Paramount Ranch on Saturday, August 18, 1956, where we were both racing. Paramount Ranch was a course designed by Ken Miles on a property then owned by Paramount Pictures just north of the San Fernando Valley where scores of movies were filmed. (It is still there, but now it's a national park, and the race track has mostly disappeared.)

Jay had entered a Lotus Mark IX he had just purchased. We seemed to hit it off, later becoming lifelong friends. He raced in a prelim to sixth overall. But then in the main event, the carburetor linkage broke in his engine and he did not finish.

As a result of taking on Lotus, Jay moved his dealership to larger quarters. During 1956, Jay raced his Mark IV in Southern California races 12 times, scoring five class wins and one first overall. At the end of the year, he drove for Colin Chapman's factory team at the Bahamas Speed Week. On December 12, 1956, he won the Preliminary Nassau Race driving a Lotus Eleven. In the Nassau Trophy Race, he finished 16th overall and first in class.

Because of his Bahamas victories, the following year Chapman entered Jay and Ignacio Lozano at Sebring in an Eleven. After a very strong run, they failed to finish. Next, Jay and MacKay-Fraser won their class at Le Mans in 1957, were second in the Index of Performance, and scored a very creditable ninth overall. As it turned out, this was Jay's best international performance. The Lotus Team, with Jay now a full-fledged member, went from Le Mans on to Rouen on July 7, 1957, where Jay was second in the Eleven. The next race was the 12 Hours of Reims where Jay had an accident, destroying the Lotus but fortunately avoiding serious injuries. MacKay-Fraser was killed during the race in another Lotus. The excitement of the Le Mans victory was over.

In 1958, it was back to Sebring again where Jay and Bill Frost were ninth overall and then on to Le Mans again in a Lotus Fifteen, this time co-driving with Pete Lovely (of Chapter 21) for a did not finish. In 1959 and 1960, Chapman switched Jay to Lotus Elites for Sebring and Le Mans.

Jay drove in Formula One for Ecurie Excelsior, a non-works Lotus team, during 1962. Debuting on July 21 at the British Grand Prix, he participated in a total of three world championship events but scored no points. In addition, he was in a number of non–Championship Formula One races. Towards the end of 1962, Jay and Chapman had a serious disagreement, and the U.S. distributorship was terminated.

When his European racing career came to an end, Jay returned to the United

Above: Herbert MacKay-Fraser (left) and Jay. According to Jay's son, Jaime, "My dad and Herbert MacKay-Fraser just after winning the 1100cc class at Le Mans in their Lotus Mk. XI. Unfortunately, MacKay-Fraser died in a racing accident a month later at Reims, France." *Below:* Jay Chamberlain in his Lotus passing through the tunnel at Pomona on February 1, 1959. Both photographs: Jay Chamberlain collection courtesy his son, Jaime.

Jay's dealership in Burbank, California, 1956. Jay Chamberlain collection courtesy of his son, Jaime.

States to manage a Porsche dealership in Florida. Jay moved to Arizona in 1967, where he purchased the Volkswagen dealership in Tucson and opened another VW dealership in Nogales. He also bought and sold a number of exotic cars at the dealerships. In 1982, he sold the dealerships and retired.

Jay occasionally raced in vintage events in his Formula Two Lotus as well as one time at the Monterey Historics in my Devin SS. In 1986, we had an open-road race across northern Baja California in Mexico. During the awards dinner Jay was the recipient of the first-ever Fabulous Fifties Lifetime Achievement Award.

Jay and his second wife, Marion, lived at their ranch near Tucson until his death in 2001. The ranch had an eclectic group of various animals, including a mule to whom Jay was devoted. It also had an extensive garage complex where Jay kept and worked on his car collection.

Jay and his former wife, Beverly, had two sons, Jaime and Jody. Jay Chamberlain was a very special person to me and we were close friends. After he moved to Arizona, we would occasionally visit back and forth as well as conduct numerous telephone conversations.

For a time, Jay lived in the South Bay area of Los Angeles where I have lived since 1965. After he sold the dealerships and retired to his ranch in Tucson, he had plans to eventually move back to Southern California. Sadly, he didn't live long enough to achieve that goal. We would have enjoyed palling around again the way we used to during the fifties.

Postscript

Colin Chapman was the designer and constructor of Lotus sports and sports-racing cars. His creations are widely raced and are popular with vintage racers.

"Chunky," as Anthony Colin Bruce Chapman was called, was born in 1928 in England. He received a degree in structural engineering from University College in London. In 1939, he served in the Royal Air Force. After World War II, he worked at the British Aluminium Company.

While working nights and weekends, Chapman built and raced his first creation, the Lotus Mark I, a modified Austin 7. Still working at British Aluminium, he designed and built his Mark II. When others wanted to buy copies, he founded his sports car company, Lotus Cars, in 1952. At first, he ran the company in his spare time assisted by a group of enthusiasts.

His design philosophy emphasized building lightweight space-framed cars with great handling characteristics. The engines were also lightweight and somewhat less powerful than his competition. Colin is quoted as saying, "Adding power makes you faster on the straights. Subtracting weight makes you faster everywhere."

Chapman's personal race driving culminated in 1956 when he participated in Formula One. Unfortunately, he crashed into Mike Hawthorn

Top: Jay at the Monterey Historic Races driving in a vintage race. Jay Chamberlain collection courtesy of his son, Jaime. *Bottom:* Jay at his home in Tucson, Arizona. Photograph by the author.

during the French Grand Prix, suffering injuries that ended his career behind the wheel.

Revolutionary at the time, Lotus cars have won a large number of races. Later cars are mid-engined and monocoque. Chapman pioneered the use of monocoque construction in 1962 with the Lotus 25. Under Colin's direction, Team Lotus won seven Formula One Constructors' titles and six Drivers' Championships. Driving a Lotus 25, Jim Clark won the Formula One Championship and then went on to win the Indy 500 in 1965.

While still racing, Lotus Cars built tens of thousands of relatively affordable sports cars for the street. Always underfinanced, Chapman was provided with money for his production by North America. Financing was made available through an agreement with Jay Chamberlain, the Lotus U.S. distributor. The first Lotus GT, the Elite, was introduced in 1957 with many more to follow.

Colin Chapman suffered a heart attack and passed away in 1982. He was 54 years old.

7

Jack McAfee

We called him "Big Jack." He was physically large but not fat. And he was big in other ways too. He had a big heart, big talent and big generosity. Jack was among that small group of fifties-era American road-racing drivers who had world-class ability. Although he sometimes competed in international events—notably Sebring and Mexico—unlike some of the others, he chose family and his business over pursuing a professional career behind the wheel.

Jack Ernest McAfee was born in San Francisco on December 21, 1922. His early years were spent in Bishop, California, but then the family moved to Hollywood, and Jack attended John Marshall High where he was right tackle on the football team. The team played in the All-City Championship Tournament at the Rose Bowl in Pasadena. The auto-shop teacher at John Marshall was so impressed with Jack's mechanical abilities that he arranged for him to start taking classes at Frank Wiggins Trade School (now LA Trade Tech) while still attending high school. This didn't last long, as Jack voluntarily joined the Navy during his senior year with the hopes of becoming an aircraft mechanic.

Jack enlisted in the Navy on September 21, 1942, and was sent for basic training in Farragut, Idaho. Afterwards, Jack had a short stint on the streets of San Francisco. He was issued a Colt .45 sidearm and became part of a shore patrol detail to help keep drunken sailors from starting bar fights etc. Shore patrol members were the Navy equivalent of Army military police. The shore patrol liked big guys. Next, he was sent to the Aviation Machinist's Mate School in Norman, Oklahoma. Then in June 1943, he served on a ship that went first to Tonga, then New Caledonia and Espiritu Santo, south of the Solomon Islands. The Navy's Seabees construction battalion had created an air base on the island that was used to launch attacks on the Japanese forces. Luganville Airfield was the staging area for Navy and Marine units, such as Greg "Pappy" Boyington's VMF 214 Black Sheep Squadron, that were moving up to Guadalcanal. After the Japanese surrendered, he returned to Coronado's North Island Naval base where he was an aircraft mechanic and achieved the rank of aviation machinist mate first class. He received an honorable discharge in January 1946, after which he enlisted in the Navy Reserve and got a final discharge on August 18, 1963.

Jack in the U.S. Navy, 1942. Jack McAfee collection.

After his 1946 discharge, he opened his own auto-repair shop. It was run out of a gas station on Pier Avenue in Hermosa Beach. Hermosa and Redondo Beach were the home of the Pacific Sports Car Club, the hottest component of the California Sports Car Club. Mary Davis and Vasek Polak were members. He had started racing hot rods and sprinters just for fun. Jack parked his Sprint car outside his shop as an attraction. When it attracted a customer, who asked about the car, Jack explained that he raced it at nearby Carrell Speedway. He invited the customer to watch the next race. The customer was Tony Parravano, who, after the race, asked McAfee how he could get involved as a sponsor.

Jack's first sports car race was, would you believe, driving Tony Parravano's 1949 convertible Cadillac at the very first Palm Springs held on April 16, 1950. Tony, for whom Jack would subsequently drive Ferraris, had entered two Cadillacs, the convertible and a sedan that Parravano drove. Parravano jumped into racing with both feet, plus body and soul! He became one of the largest owner-sponsors of Italian sports racers in the United States. It all came to naught when the Internal Revenue Service pushed Humpty Dumpty off the wall. Parravano's stable ended up in an abandoned chicken barn in Van Nuys, California. The sight of a 450S Maserati and numerous Ferraris stuffed into rows of cubicles still containing the residue of a chicken farm operation was something to behold! The IRS tried to keep the auction secret to protect their regular buyers. A few of us showed up and the 450S Maserati sold for about ten grand. The pro auctioneers tried to keep outsiders from getting any of the cars. One of the pros said, "If you guys hadn't showed up, I could have got the car for two grand and let you have it for five."

Tony, wanted by the FBI for jumping bail, had disappeared in 1960 and is still the subject of the biggest conspiracy theory on the Southern California sports car scene.

Before his legal troubles began, Parravano selected Jack to drive his Tipo 340 Ferrari America in the November 1952 Carrera Panamericana. Ernie McAfee (no relation to Jack) was the navigator, and they came in fifth overall.

Jack gave up his shop and went to work as a mechanic for Ernie McAfee, who had a race shop near Hollywood. There he became acquainted with John Von Neumann, whose Porsche-VW distributorship was located on Vine Street in Hollywood. In 1952, at age 29, Jack became one of the first Porsche-VW dealers. He set up shop in the San

Jack McAfee drove his own MG Special at Palm Springs in 1951. Jack McAfee collection.

Fernando Valley and continued until 1974, when he sold out and went to work with Porsche Factory Racing as a consultant for the next ten years.

Jack remembered racing for Parravano. I'll let him tell it as he told it to me in his own words:

> In 1954, I started driving a 4.5 Ferrari for Tony Parravano. The car was notorious for not having any brakes. The brake drums were aluminum with steel linings. When the brakes got hot, the aluminum [that] Ferrari had used would expand to such an extent that the steel linings didn't have any backing and the shoes wouldn't grip properly. As a result, I had to learn how to drive the car without using the brakes. After the first application, the pedal would just go to the floor. So I had to use the gears to slow down for corners.
>
> We took the car to San Francisco for the June 5, 1954, Golden Gate race. As I look back on it, I realize now how dangerous it was. If you got off the course almost anywhere, you were in trouble. There were many beautiful trees, quite a few of which were near the course. In some places, there was a ditch alongside the road. If you slid off and got two wheels in the ditch, over you would go.
>
> A lot of good cars and drivers were entered in the main event. At the start, Chuck Daigh in his Kurtis-Chrysler took the lead followed by George Sawyer in another Kurtis and then me in the 4.5.

Above: Jack's shop on Pier Avenue in Hermosa Beach, California, 1949. Jack McAfee collection.

Left: (From left) Pat McAfee, Jack's first wife; Ron Parravano, the young son of Jack's car owner Tony; Phil Hill; and Jack celebrate Jack's winning the 1954 Golden Gate race. Jack McAfee collection.

On the fifth lap, I was able to take over the lead. At that point, I hadn't used the brakes at all, and I knew I could make one good stop before the drums got too hot. Bill Stroppe [see Chapter 20], in his Mercury-Kurtis, driving very hard, had come up behind me. All of a sudden, BAM, he nerfed me. I don't think he did it intentionally; it was just done in the heat of the race. Then we started into a long, downhill straight stretch followed by a sharp corner, Bill was right on my tail. I went into the corner as deep as I possibly could and used my one time on the brakes. I don't know how good the brakes were on the Kurtis, but when I glanced into the rear-view mirror, there was Stroppe with his nose buried in the hay bales. That was it; I was out of brakes. But it was essentially the end of the race. From then on, nobody got anywhere near me.

For quite a few years, Jack drove Porsches for Vasek Polak. In 1956, Jack won the under-two-liter SCCA National Championship, a feat he repeated in 1958 and again in 1960. His last race (except for vintage) was in 1962 at Pomona on July 22 when he drove an RSK Porsche to second place in the main event, behind Bill Krause in a Birdcage Maserati.

In 1958, *Road & Track* listed McAfee as one of the top nine sports car drivers in America. In 1951, he was the Pacific Coast Champion in the under-two-liter class; in

Jack drove Vasek Polak's Porsche Spyder (no. 88) to third place in the Semi-Main event at Palm Springs on November 2, 1956. John Kunstle is the 118 car, also a Porsche Spyder. Jack McAfee collection.

Jack won 50 races between 1950 and 1962. This photograph was taken at Pebble Beach, California, in 1955. Jack McAfee collection.

1956, the National Champion in under-two-liters; in 1958 and again in 1960, he won the under-two-liter crown again. As a true amateur, Jack sometimes ventured outside California for pro events, and he finished among the top ten at both the 12 Hours of Sebring and the Mexican Road Race.

One thing that set Jack apart in those days from the rest of us in Southern California was that he became involved with SCCA governance at the national level. Among other positions, he served on the National Contest Board. His purpose and primary interest was safety. Jack pioneered the use of such things as fireproof clothing, roll bars and adequate harnesses.

McAfee was also concerned with course design. Because of Jack's insistence, Laguna Seca is run counterclockwise rather than the initially planned European manner. Imagine running clockwise up the hill to the Corkscrew and then speeding down that long slope into a fast right-hand sweeper with no runoff! I wonder how many lives Jack saved.

In the late eighties, I restored my old MG Special and entered it in the Monterey Historics. Initially, I was going to drive, but when I got to thinking about it, I asked Jack if he would like to have one last go and he agreed. I thought it appropriate since one of his first rides was in an MG Special. This was the first occasion that Jack had been to Laguna Seca since racing for real. A large number of entrants and spectators remembered him and stopped by our paddock to say hello and reminisce.

John Dixon prepped my MG for Jack before we went to Monterey. We took it to Willow Springs for testing. John remarked,

> Jack and I had been forties Southern California hot rodders and had that early days' camaraderie. On the way home from Willow, Jack seemed somber. I asked him, "What's the matter? That puny MG not big enough?" Jack replied, "Hardly that. I used to drive a race car as easily as zipping my fly. But after all these years, I have had to be conscious of every move!"

Jack and I were good friends since we served together on the board of directors of the Los Angeles Region of the Sports Car Club of America.

After Jack retired in 1984 he went to live in a Seal Beach retirement community where he stayed very active. Until grounded by a hip problem, he and I used to take bicycle rides together. Jack rode almost every morning. And a couple of times every week he went ballroom dancing. He also enjoyed fishing. I called him "Action." (As in "Action Jackson!") Until Jack passed away, we would have lunch together about once a month at our favorite restaurant in Seal Beach.

Quiet and unassuming, Jack McAfee, with world-championship-level ability, was respected by everyone in the racing community, not only as an outstanding driver but also as a great sportsman.

Many of those who knew Jack and knew about his ability have wondered why he didn't pursue a professional career as a race driver. Perhaps his son, Rex, has the answer. In 1999, he wrote me a letter about his dad.

"Big Jack" had a big heart, big talent and big generosity. Jack McAfee collection.

Jack at Seal Beach in 1990. Photograph by the author.

The one thing my dad put above everything in racing was the need to have fun. Driving the big Ferraris and dealing with wealthy team owners eventually all fell by the wayside and, in the end, left him with his friend, Harry Jones, to trailer a Lotus up and down the coast in 1961 when he won the Pacific Coast Formula Junior Championship.

On March 10, 2007, we lost one of America's early sports car pioneers and a truly great driver. Jack died at age 84. Jack is survived by his ex-wife Gerry, their son, Rex (named after Rex Mays), and a daughter, Mimi, who has a daughter and son. Interment was private.

8

Ken Miles

In the United States during the fifties, there were a number of road racing drivers who went on to international success during the next decade. Phil Hill, Carroll Shelby, and Dan Gurney come immediately to mind. However, if a single fifties-era dominating figure had to be chosen, it would be Ken Miles. And during the sixties, he became the preeminent engineer at Shelby American. He brought to America the European concept of sports car racing, club organization, and road race car construction.

Ken was an important figure with an imposing personality, particularly in Southern California. He was not only one of the top road-racing pilots, but he also designed courses, devised rules, set schedules and helped govern the California Sports Car Club (in those days, independent from the Sports Car Club of America). In addition, he was an excellent writer, contributing many articles to motorsports magazines.

Kenneth Henry Miles was born in Sutton Coldfield, England, in November 1918 at the house of his grandfather, a tea and coffee importer. As a child, Ken's interests lay chiefly in taking his toys apart to see how and why they worked and in building complicated mechanical devices. But during his school days he was a dead loss as a scholar. Like many geniuses, such as Edison and Tesla, his hands couldn't be separated from his intellect while he sat in a classroom.

At 11 years old, Ken's interests were beginning to be centered on motor bikes and cars. When he was 15, he was introduced by a friend to a couple of high school girls. After the meeting he said to his friend about one of them, named Mollie, "I'm going to marry that girl." To this end, Ken applied himself with such single mindedness that his headmaster finally phoned his parents to plead, "Can't you do something about this Mollie business?" His parents duly wasted much breath on this project, but Ken continued wooing, working intermittently on the building of an Austin 7 Special named Nellie. This little car had a modified induction and exhaust system and a higher-than-standard compression ratio. The little car was a great success and was finally sold during World War II. When last heard of, it was still going strong.

After he left school at age 16, Ken was apprenticed to Wolseley Motors, where he slowly worked his way through every phase of automobile production, from sweeping the floor on up. For transport, he rode a Velocette motorbike, which he was forced to sell when he lost his driving license for a year because of his speeding.

World War II started in September 1939. Ken was called up and was in camp with the Territorial Army and was immediately posted to an anti-aircraft unit located in the chief armament producing area of England. When Coventry was destroyed during the Blitz he saw plenty of excitement. But the highlight of his sojourn there was his marriage to Mollie. Next was a transfer to the newly formed Royal Corps of Electrical and Mechanical Engineers, where he took a course in engineering and maintenance of military vehicles. Emerging from this with the highest marks of any student, he finished the course and achieved the rank of staff sergeant, Ken was posted to a tank unit on the east coast. After several more postings throughout England and Scotland, Ken joined the invasion of Europe on D-Day plus two.

Ken saw service in Normandy, France, Holland, Belgium and Germany, working on tank reconnaissance and recovery, frequently a very gruesome job. When a German 88 penetrated a tank's armor, it left the crew splattered around on the inside. Recovered tanks had to be cleaned and refitted. Ken's was the first British unit to pass through the notorious concentration camp at Bergen-Belsen, a doubly gruesome experience. When the war ended, he was stationed on the Baltic coast of Germany where he spent his off-duty time organizing motorcycle races and sailing yachts. Ken was noted for his profile and imposing personality. During his military career, his prominent nose suffered a few adjustments.

Ken was discharged from the Army in January 1946 after nearly seven years' service. Soon thereafter he bought a Frazer-Nash. It was all light alloy, and after Ken had inserted a Ford V8 engine, it went like the proverbial bat out of hell. He ran it with some success in hill climbs at Prescott and Shelsley Walsh and also in club events at the Silverstone circuit. It was probably at this time that he began to be noticed as a driver.

He returned to Wolseley Motors, where he was engaged for some time in toolmaking. However, there seemed little chance for advancement, and when he was asked to join a friend in the production of race cars, the temptation was quite irresistible. The race car in question was a 500cc originally designed by Paul Emery with front-wheel drive and rubber cord suspension. The overall dry weight

Ken, shown here in 1940, was a sergeant in the British army during World War II.

was 475 pounds. Ken loved every minute of this work, but it was very exacting, since it was necessary for him to spend about 100 hours a week on the project in order to carry out their order on schedule. After several months, the long hours and lack of sleep took quite a heavy toll on his health, and he lost 14 pounds, getting very nervous and run down.

About this time Ken was offered a job with Gough Industries in California by John Beazley, then general manager of Gough, an importer and distributor of British cars. Beazley came from Ken's hometown and had worked at Wolseley. He needed a service manager and Ken fit the bill. Ken left England just before Christmas 1951 and took up his post at Gough, where he felt quite at home and happy. Soon, Ken began entering sports car races, running a stock MGTD at first and later an MG Mark II. Before long, he was working on the production of an MG Special (R-1). The design was entirely his own, and apart from the engine, the car was composed solely of stock MG and Morris components. Its first race was the 1953 Pebble Beach, then the preeminent—and most hotly contested—western states event. When Ken arrived there, he had had absolutely no opportunity to test the car. Even so, he won the main event for

The first MG special Ken Miles built was called R1. In 1953, the year this photograph was taken, he won every race he entered in it. Ken Miles collection.

cars under 1500cc and then went on to win every single event he entered that year, a total of ten races, an astonishing feat.

The next year—1954—he sold the R-1 to Cy Yedor and started to work on its successor, R-2. This second car was innovative for its time, with a very lightweight frame constructed of small tubes and an aerodynamic envelope body. In 1955, Ken won Pebble Beach in the R-2, while Yedor came in third in an R-1. By then, Ken had become known as Mr. MG. During that same year, he was elected to the first of three terms as president of the California Sports Car Club. He designed three of the courses we used—Bakersfield, Pomona and Paramount Ranch—and put together a program of a race almost every month. Undoubtedly this contributed to the success of a number of our local drivers, because they got more seat time than those less fortunate who lived in other locales.

I first met Ken at the July 3–4, 1954, road races at Torrey Pines. Ken had just sold his first MG Special—R-1—to Cy Yedor, who won the under–1500cc modified event that weekend in it. Ken won the main event—the over–1500cc modified—in the Troutman-Barnes Special powered by a flathead Ford V8.

Ken driving a production MG at Torrey Pines on October 22, 1955. Ken Miles collection.

8. Ken Miles

My off-and-on hobby-profession is photography. I was out on Turn Two with my Rolleiflex camera. Turn Two was a sharp right-hander for which the drivers had to slow considerably. It was very near a cliff that dropped off to rocks on the Pacific shore. If a car missed the turn—and occasionally some did—the consequences were dire.

The main event was one hour long, and Ken had built up a considerable lead towards the end. I was drinking a Coke. Apparently, Ken was thirsty because on one lap he stopped and gestured to me to hand him the Coke, which I did. The next lap he stopped again and handed back the empty bottle. In later years, of course, he would have been disqualified for such an infraction. But in those days, things were more relaxed. After the race, I strolled down to the pits, struck up a conversation with Ken and we became lifelong friends. He was also my hero.

After a little more than four years on the job, Ken was fired as the result of a disagreement with the boss, Phil Gough, Sr.

Next Ken went to work for Clem Atwater, who had a major foreign car dealership in the San Fernando Valley. This job lasted only a few months. Ken quit and went to work for John Von Neumann's Competition Motors, western states Porsche-VW dis-

(Left to right) John Von Neumann, Dick Van Laanan, an unidentified man, Ken, and Ken's wife Mollie at Torrey Pines in 1956. Ken drove Porsches successfully for Von Neumann. Ken Miles Collection.

tributor. Ken performed a number of functions, the most important of which was racing John's 550 Porsche Spyders. Driving a Spyder for Von Neumann during 1956 and 1957, Ken won first overall 16 times. His most successful time with Von Neumann, however, was at the wheel of a Cooper. With a Porsche four-cam racing engine in place of the usual Climax, Ken won seven out of nine races entered, including a first in class and fourth overall at Nassau against the best the world had to offer. The Porsche people in Germany became upset and forced Von Neumann to sell the Cooper.

As the result of a dispute with Von Neumann at the end of 1957, Ken joined the Otto Zipper–Bob Estes team with which he continued through 1966 driving Porsches. All in all, with this marque, Ken achieved 38 first-place finishes and almost always stood on the podium.

After another short stint selling cars for another dealer, Ken opened his own repair shop, Ken Miles Limited, in North Hollywood.

During that time, Ken occasionally raced a Sunbeam Alpine for Rootes Motors. Jack Brabham said of it, "What a great car if it only had power." In 1963, Rootes thought a 260 Ford V8 would fit and do the trick. They delivered engineless Alpines to both Carroll Shelby and Ken Miles. The first conversion was completed by Ken in only one weekend.

Unfortunately, Ken was a much better driver and mechanic than a businessman. One day his employees came to work to find that the IRS had padlocked the door. Ken went to work for Shelby as competition manager. Until then, Cobras had been raced but without much success. With Ken doing the preparation, Cobras placed first and second at Riverside on February 3, 1963. Ken let Dave MacDonald win and he finished second. Ken went on to drive in more races for Shelby than any other team member. His record was also better than any of the others.

According to Shelby,

> Ken was unique. It seemed like he created a hell of a lot of controversy before he came to work for me. But we always got along just fine; he was the heart and soul of our testing program. He made the Daytona Coupe work. Ken was a world-class driver. He was also helpful to the other drivers on my team. He reminded me of Fangio in that regard. In the years before Shelby American, we knew him as kind of a hothead, but it never showed up during the time he was with me.

Ken's personality was anathema to wannabe types and their shallow posturing.

During 1963, Ken was entered in a Cobra 16 times, winning three and placing second in six. That same year, Ken drove for Zipper-Estes five times, winning two and placing second in two. The following year, he won ten events in a Cobra.

The next year—1965—Shelby American took over the Ford effort to prepare and campaign GT-40s. The first time out was Daytona, where Ken and Lloyd Ruby won the 24 Hours. At Sebring, he and Bruce McLaren were second overall, and they were third at Monza in Italy. Ford became a serious contender for the World Manufacturers' Championship.

The fateful year was 1966, the time of Shelby's and Ken's greatest triumphs and, of course, an unspeakable tragedy. In those days, the triple crown of road racing was

8. Ken Miles

Ken would have won the 1966 Le Mans, but he held back and took second. Bruce McLaren won and Ronnie Buckman came in third. Shelby collection, courtesy Tracey Smith.

the 24 Hours of Daytona, the 12 Hours of Sebring and, the granddaddy of them all, the 24 Hours of Le Mans. Ken, with co-driver Lloyd Ruby, won both Daytona and Sebring. Daytona was a clean-sweep for Shelby with his GT-40s taking first, second and third.

Towards the end of the 24 Hours of Le Mans, it became rather obvious that the Shelby MkII GT-40s would win. Ken, with co-driver Denny Hulme, was leading with the Bruce McLaren–Chris Amon car second and a third GT-40, driven by Ronnie Bucknum and Dick Hutcherson, some 60 miles behind in third.

At the last pit stop for the three leading cars, the drivers were informed that Henry Ford II (the "Deuce") had decided it would be good publicity for all three to finish in a dead heat. Both Ken and Shelby objected, saying that this would be unfair to Ken and Denny. Actually, a dead heat with all three cars crossing the finish line at the same time was impossible. According to the rules, the car that travels the farthest distance wins. Since the cars don't start together, but rather are lined up in a row along the pit wall, if the first car and the second car at the start and finish ends in a dead heat, the second car would be the winner having traveled about ten feet farther. If Ken and McLaren were to cross the line exactly together, McLaren would be the winner because the McLaren-Amon car was lined up behind the Miles-Hulme car at the start.

At any rate, after receiving the instructions, Ken slowed down for McLaren's car and then both slowed so that Bucknum could catch up. The Deuce got a picture that was flashed around the world! Ken, angry and disconsolate from being deprived of the triple crown, slowed slightly just before the finish line, allowing McLaren to take the checkered flag first. The official results show that McLaren-Amon traveled 0.020 kilometers farther than Miles-Hulme.

I had dinner with Ken and his wife, Mollie, two months later, and he seemed resigned to accepting the unacceptable result. He was looking forward to bigger and better things and was convinced his driving career had not yet peaked.

Meanwhile, the Ford Motor Company was developing a successor to the GT-40s called the "J" car. Ken was scheduled to test the prototype at Riverside for Shelby, who was conducting the program for Ford. On August 16, 1966, he unofficially broke the record with a lap of 1 minute, 26.4 seconds. Two days later on August 18, going some 180 mph, the car went off the bank at the end of the long back straight, bounced end over end and caught fire. The car was totally destroyed, and Ken lost his life.

I was in Mexico City on a photo assignment when my dad called me at my hotel at four in the morning to tell me what had happened. The Miles family and mine were close friends. My dad and Ken were best friends as were my stepmother and Mollie.

Ken (left) and Lloyd Ruby won the 1966 Sebring for Shelby. Shelby collection, courtesy Tracey Smith.

My father, Art Evans Sr. (right), and Ken were best friends. This photograph was taken in Pasadena in 1958. Photograph by Art Evans.

Mollie insisted that my dad deliver the eulogy, and during the call, we talked about what he would say. Unfortunately, I couldn't get back in time for the service.

According to journalist Jim Crow, Ken had an ability to alienate people and was sometimes his own worst enemy. But with Shelby, everything seemed to go right. Both were champion drivers deeply involved with the development of cars. Carroll and Ken had a rapport based on mutual respect and admiration.

Mollie Miles died in 1973. She left her son, Peter, who lives in Monterey, California. One time Peter told me, "When my dad was killed, we were right at the point when we were just starting to transition from a father-son relationship to becoming friends. So I really miss that feeling of knowing him as a friend. I wish I could have had that experience."

9

Jim Peterson

Jim Peterson is best remembered as the person who designed and built Riverside International Raceway. This course was the premier Southern California venue for road racing. A number of premier events were held there, such as Formula One, Can-Am, Trans-Am and so forth. James Edward Peterson was born in Buena Park, California, on May 26, 1925.

His father, Edward, was born in Redmond, Wisconsin, in 1891. His mother, Jennie Caroline Madsen, was born in Copenhagen, Denmark, in 1899. Jim grew up in Riverside, California, on his parents' farm where watermelons were grown. Jim's job was to stand guard at night keeping the coyotes away with his single-shot .22 rifle. His dad was also a carpenter. Jim learned the trade working with his father.

In Riverside High School, Jim excelled in auto shop. He was to use that talent throughout his racing career.

When Jim was 16 years old, the Japanese attacked Pearl Harbor, and we were at war. When he turned 18, Jim joined the Army. After basic training, he was assigned to the Army Air Corps to become a pilot. First, he was sent to the Hammer Army Airfield near Fresno, California, where he was trained to fly in a Piper J3. Afterwards he was sent to Pensacola, Florida, for further training in a Stearman PT-17. Upon completion, he got his wings and was commissioned as a second lieutenant. Next, he trained to be a troop glider pilot. It was a daredevil and dangerous new way to transport troops.

Called "the Flying Coffins of WWII," they were unarmed Waco CG-4A combat gliders. These were primitive aircraft, made of tubing, canvas and plywood with no engines. They were powered only by wind and the courage of the men who flew them. They were silent—the element of surprise—and they could land on rough terrain. Towed into the air by C-47s, they were employed during D-Day to augment the invasion of Europe. This method of landing troops behind enemy lines was more efficient than by parachute. Each carried thirteen troops and their equipment. Enemy fire as the gliders descended was often intense. After landing the troops, the pilots and copilots had to walk back, making their way through enemy lines, a perilous journey in itself. Forty percent of the pilots didn't come back. Jim, however, survived, and when the war was over, he was awarded the Army Air Medal and discharged.

Jim met his wife while he was in the Army Air Corps. She was born Marjorie Steen in Anaheim, California. She played the pipe organ in the local Presbyterian church.

Talented with his hands, Jim got a number of construction jobs and became a jack-of-all-trades. Eventually, he formed J. E. Peterson, General Contractor with offices and an equipment yard in Pasadena. He built quite a number of structures during the fifties, mostly in the Pasadena area.

After acquiring an XK120 Jaguar, he started to campaign it in West Coast amateur road races. He ended up winning so many races that he became known as the "Jag Master." A shelf in his home was filled with trophies. The record shows that he raced starting in 1954 and continued through 1957. During that time, he was in 28 events, won 4 overall and won his class 11 times.

Even though he undoubtedly had the talent, because of his successful business he couldn't spend any really serious time at the sport. An exception was Sebring. For two years, 1956 and 1957, he was a team driver for the Arnolt-Bristol team at Sebring. And also he won Class D in the Mobilgas Economy Run driving a Studebaker Hawk in 1960.

I was racing a rather tired XK120 at the time. Most of us in the over-1500cc production group came to know one another. The group included Rudy Cleye in his 300SL. Rudy was the visionary who conceived the idea of a raceway near Riverside. When initial financing dried up, Rudy convinced wealthy sportsman John Edgar to put up the necessary construction funds. Rudy selected Jim Peterson as the general contractor.

In 1956, Chevrolet replaced the original six-cylinder Corvette with one featuring a V8 engine. A dealer or the factory—I don't know which—employed Jim to prepare and race the new model. This was the first time a Corvette had been in serious competition on the West Coast. There was a lot of debugging yet to do—which Jim was very good at—and Jim's contribution helped in the car's later success.

After the 1956 season, Jim retired from racing at the insistence of his wife, Margie, and he sold the Jaguar to me. Jim raced again in only one event. The occasion was the 1957 Palm Springs SCCA National. Jim had been appointed race chairman, and I was his assistant. We went early in the week to set up the course. Jim's wife planned on coming for Sunday only. I had entered the ex-Peterson XK120. Saturday was a short five-lapper to determine Sunday's starting positions. As we were lining up at the pre-grid, I called to Jim, "Hey, Jim, why don't you give it a go one last time. Margie will never know!" He agreed, put on my helmet, and got behind the wheel.

The *Sports Car Journal* reported, "Saturday's over-1500 production race got off to a flashing start.... The big surprise of this event was the return of old Jag-Master, Jim Peterson. Jim tooled Art Evans' XK120 to a magnificent third, in front of Mercedes, Corvettes, Ace Bristols, etc. In fact, he had a battle with Ron Ellico for his spot that may have been the high point of the afternoon." Actually, Jim was gaining on the leaders and, had the race been longer than five laps, probably would have won.

When the Riverside International Raceway project came along, before starting construction, Jim spent a few months in Europe touring various courses. During the trip, he visited the Jaguar factory at Coventry where he purchased one of the few XKSS cars that had been made before the fire at the factory destroyed the tooling.

When Jim and the car arrived back in California, he would occasionally drive the car to and from his home and the Riverside site, a round-trip of about 130 miles. As time allowed, I would accompany Jim, riding in the left-hand passenger seat. At the site, Jim used a surplus U.S. Army Jeep—often with me in the right-hand seat—around the property planning the course layout. Although others have claimed credit, I know from personal experience that Jim not only built the track but also designed it.

In those days, the raceway site was located near a highway (U.S. 395) that went from Riverside to San Diego. (It still does, but now it's a freeway.) The property for the raceway was just north of March Air Force Base, where we had raced in 1953 and 1954, courtesy of General Curtis LeMay. Just south of the base, Highway 395 was long and straight.

One day Jim told me, "I want to see just how fast this thing will go." So we started off down the highway. After we passed the base, he floored the loud pedal. In the XKSS, the tachometer was in front of the driver and the speedometer in front of the passenger. So here I was, looking at the speedo as well as traffic going the other way. Soon we were passing cars going our way as if they were standing still and the needle started to approach its limit, 180 mph. Even at that speed, I don't remember much wind buffeting and the car seemed rock steady. I was supposed to tell Jim when the needle reached 180. When I did, he backed off, turned around and drove sedately back. Afterwards Jim remarked that he didn't believe the speedo was accurate because of tire expansion.

Occasionally, Jim would drive his XKSS around his quiet residential neighborhood. To put it mildly, this attracted some attention, often from a gendarme. When a patrol car would set off after Jim, he would speed away. But the problem was that the officers knew where he lived. A friend—Dr. John Valentine—lived across town. Dr. Valentine was an SCCA official. Jim had an arrangement with Dr. Valentine to leave his garage door open with an empty space. When a patrol car got after him, Jim would get far enough ahead so the officer couldn't see him, then drive into the Valentine garage and close the door. This tactic caused great glee among local sports car aficionados. One night though, Jim had to spend the entire night with the Valentines when the police kept looking for him.

When the Riverside course was completed, Jim in his XKSS led a procession of cars around for the very first lap. This time I wasn't in the passenger seat because I was taking pictures. (The following year, Jim sold the car to Steve

Jim Peterson in the backyard of the Peterson home in Altadena in 1959. Photograph by the author.

McQueen.) The first race was held by the California Sports Car Club on September 21–22, 1957. On Sunday the 22nd, the first race was for production cars under 1500cc. A friend of Jim's and mine lost his life in his MG on Turn Six. This put a pall on what should have been a great day. The funeral was held in the same Pasadena Presbyterian church where Jim Peterson's dad had been buried a few years before. This was my second experience at box carrying. Not only that, while racing in the main event, my friend Carroll Shelby ran into a dirt bank and was ferried to the hospital with face cuts that required 70 stitches. John Edgar's brand-new $20,000 4.5 Maserati was badly bent. Turn Six was banked on the inside and flat and dirty on the outer half. Joe Weatherly was killed there in a NASCAR race.

A bitter conflict in Southern California had developed between the Los Angeles Region and the then independent California Sports Car Club. The issue was that there were not enough venues in the area and not enough weekends for both clubs. Things started to come to a head in 1961. The chain that pulled the plug was an accident at an SCCA Pomona event on July 9, 1961, when one spectator was killed and 14 injured. Jim Peterson, who had been elected regional executive of the sponsoring Sports Car Club

The new Riverside Raceway was completed in 1956. Jim Peterson (left) is on the grid for the first lap next to Ken Miles (center) and Jay Chamberlain. Steve Peterson collection.

of America Los Angeles Region, was also the race chairman. Numerous lawsuits ensued. The accident occurred when Bob Drake, driving Old Yeller, dropped a wheel off the road in the sweeping Turn Seven and went into the crowd. The high mound at that point had been removed, which left spectators unprotected.

The LA Region of the SCCA had been having some serious differences with those who governed the SCCA National at Westport, Connecticut, for some time. The Pomona incident was the last straw and finally, on November 24, 1961, SCCA National (undoubtedly hoping to extricate itself from lawsuits) revoked the LA Region charter and offered it to the Cal Club. On November 25, the Cal Club board voted unanimously to accept the offer. This created a furor in both camps and a bitter conflict ensued that lasted for all of 1962.

Incensed, Jim demanded a hearing before the SCCA National board as specified in the bylaws. Failing that, he threatened an injunction that would tie up racing in Southern California. Jim and many LA Region members determined to continue business as usual and scheduled a race at Palm Springs for January 1962 and one at Pomona in March. SCCA National threatened legal action to require the LA Region to "disassociate itself from SCCA and desist from using their name and insignia," whereupon the group, a California corporation, associated itself with the then professional sanctioning body, the U.S. Auto Club. The defunct LA Region changed its name to the U.S. Sports Car Club, a division of the USAC, with Jim its president. The battle continued between the California Sports Car Club Region of the SCCA and the USSCC for the few available Southern California courses, with both clubs scheduling events for 1962. The leadership of each threatened to ban drivers who participated in the other club's races. This caused quite a stir among those of us who raced, as most of us belonged to both clubs.

USSCC president Jim Peterson, along with the Pomona Elks Club, scheduled a race at Pomona for July 21 and 22, 1962. In an unexpected move and with the threat of a drivers' boycott (which would have been a financial disaster for both), the USSCC and the Cal Club decided to merge. While the details were being worked out, the Cal Club threw its weight behind the Pomona event. Before racing started, the two club presidents, Jim and Cal Club president D. D. Michelmore, paraded around the track together in the course car to the cheers of the drivers. But some observers noted that neither looked very happy, particularly Michelmore. After the race, both Jim and Michelmore stepped down and the merger came about.

Jim was the general contractor for a condo complex called Laguna Royale. Somehow the project became involved in lawsuits that lasted for five years. It took a heavy toll on Jim and destroyed his business. Perhaps as a result, he became an alcoholic and was in and out of rehab programs for years. Eventually, his wife left him.

In 1977, he died of cirrhosis of the liver. He left two sons, Stephen and Kenneth, and a daughter, Cynthia. A few weeks before his death, he called me at my office. I asked how he spent his days. He had lost his driving license and didn't even have a car. He lived by himself in a very small apartment in Altadena, a few blocks from the palatial mansion where his family used to live. He said he would get up in the morning, walk a few blocks to a nearby liquor store, buy a quart of vodka and take it home and drink it.

At the time when Jim was in the hospital, his son Steve was in Denmark studying for his degree in architecture. According to Steve, "Even though I was a broke student, I returned from Denmark when he needed me. I loved my dad very much."

Jim and I were best friends. For some time during the fifties, I was single and would have dinner something like two or even three evenings every week at the Peterson home in Altadena. His family—Jim, his wife Margie and their two boys—were my surrogate family. We socialized and went on trips together. Even after all these years, I tear up when I think about Jim.

Note: My thanks to Jim's son J. Stephen Peterson, who provided me with a lot of information about his father that I didn't know.

10

Vasek Polak

When Porsche introduced the four-cam racing engine in 1953, it became a sensation. Porsche Spyders with this engine soon dominated their class. The problem was that the type 547 engine's complexity with twin overhead camshafts on each bank of the flat-four required nine shafts, 14 bevel gears and 2 spur gears to operate. It could take a highly trained technician at least 120 hours to rebuild this engine. In the United States, one man emerged who was acknowledged as a genius with the four-cam. He was Vasek Polak.

Vasek ("Va-shek"), however, was a lot more than a mechanic. He built a life that a boy who grew up in Europe, ravaged by World War I and then a worldwide depression, couldn't have imagined. It turned out to be the American dream.

Vasek was my friend and neighbor. One evening over glasses of wine, he told my family and me about his time in Czechoslovakia. (Now it's the Czech Republic.) He was born on September 11, 1914, in Prague. After graduating from high school and three years of technical school, he had a four-year apprenticeship at the Skoda factory. Vasek served in the Czech Air Force from 1935 until the German invasion in 1939.

During the German occupation, Vasek was a member of the underground. Towards the end of the war, there was an uprising in Prague against the Nazis. While trying to save a friend, Vasek was shot by a German in a tank. The bullet pierced both his lungs. Gravely wounded, he lay in a street gutter for two days until his sister found him and brought him home, where he slowly recovered.

After the war ended in 1945, Vasek operated a machine shop in Prague with 45 employees. For pleasure and transportation, he rode a 250cc motorcycle that he raced. For safekeeping during the day, he kept the bike in a box. The events he entered were 100-kilometer heats for each class: 250cc, 350cc and the largest, 500cc. A 250cc heat winner could race in the 350cc and so on. Sometimes he would race a total of 300 kilometers in a single day. He went on to win the Czechoslovak 250cc National Championship.

After the war, he continued his underground struggle, now against the Communists. Eventually, his activities became known. One day in 1948, the secret police came to arrest him. His wife, Jindriska, called on the phone to warn him, using a pre-arranged signal. She asked him when he was going to come home for lunch. That was the signal, as Vasek never went home for lunch. As the police approached the front door of his shop, he ran out the rear, jumped on his motorcycle and rode towards the west.

Disguising himself as a farmer, Vasek walked through the woods toward the West German border. Needless to say, it was a harrowing journey and he was always in danger of being discovered and shot. He managed to crawl under the wire and arrived with nothing but a torn shirt on his back. Sadly, he had had to leave his wife and children behind.

Vasek ended up in a refugee camp near Munich. Soon he got a job as a mechanic heading up the motor pool for the Red Cross and the American Consulate. Next, he became a partner in a VW-Porsche shop in Munich. He wanted to come to America with the idea that there could be opportunities that would enable him to make enough money to try to get his family out of Czechoslovakia.

With everything he had managed to save, he booked a passage to New York in 1956. Arriving with $300, he slept on a volleyball court at the Czech Community Center. Soon he landed a job with Max Hoffman repairing Porsches. He was so good at it that Hoffman sent him with teams to eastern U.S. sports car races.

My close friend Jack McAfee told me he met Vasek during a race at Beverly, Massachusetts. Vasek spoke very little English then. According to Jack, "We discussed the possibility of him moving to the West Coast. I explained that we needed someone with his knowledge and skills on Porsches, particularly the four-cam racing engine."

In 1957, Vasek decided to make the move. Towing his Porsche Spyder behind his VW van, he somehow ended up at Paramount Ranch (a now defunct road course near Los Angeles) in a California Sports Car Club race on December 7. Even though he was not entered, he was allowed a post entry under his Czech first name, Jaelav. The flags were explained during the Saturday morning drivers' meeting. With his limited English, Vasek didn't fully understand and retired from the Saturday race soon after the start. According to the official results, "[The driver] failed to understand flags, and pulled into pits." On Sunday, however, he was able to finish seventh overall and fifth in class, three laps behind the winner, Ken Miles. I remember it well because I was there racing my XK120, and I made Vasek's acquaintance in the paddock.

With $3,000 he had saved working for Hoffman, Vasek opened a Porsche repair shop in Hermosa Beach. According to McAfee, who was driving then for John Edgar and later for Stan Sugarman, "As soon as Vasek arrived, I made arrangements for him to take care of the Porsches our teams were racing. Before Vasek, I never extended the four-cam engines for fear of having to overhaul one. With Polak taking care of them, I found I could extend the rpms to much higher limits without having to worry."

At a February 1958 race at Pomona, Vasek was wrenching on Sugarman's Porsche RS Spyder driven by Jack, who won the event for modified cars under 1500cc. In a race report, Myra Jones noted that on Saturday "Betty Shutes was pretty unhappy when she discovered her engine had a cracked head and broken cam finger. Vasek took the car to his shop in Hermosa Beach and worked until 4 a.m., then towed it back to Pomona." Betty won the Ladies' Race on Sunday.

Vasek Polak in his Porsche Spyder (no. 210) being passed by Ken Miles in the race at Paramount Ranch in 1957. Vasek Polak collection.

Jack McAfee driving Vasek Polak's 917 Porsche at Riverside International Raceway in 1971. Vasek Polak collection.

Stan Sugarman entered Vasek in the novice race at Riverside on June 28–29, 1958. Even though the event included all classes, Vasek finished second overall, behind Richard Corband in the Morgenson Special. Too valuable as a mechanic, he now concluded his U.S. racing career.

Vasek and McAfee became close friends. Jack obtained a visa to travel to Czechoslovakia in order to visit the Polaks. Vasek, of course, couldn't go, as he would have been arrested. Jack took the family some money and shot some photographs so Vasek could see what his children looked like.

Western Porsche-VW distributor John Von Neumann was entering Porsche Spyders with Ken Miles and Richie Ginther driving against Jack McAfee and others at the time. John was so impressed with Vasek's ability that he had Vasek take care of his four-cams.

Wanting to expand his business, Vasek—through the influence of Von Neumann and McAfee—was able to obtain a Porsche dealership at his Hermosa Beach location in 1959. In addition, his shop was designated a special outlet for Porsche racing parts. In 1966, Vasek took a 911 off his showroom floor and prepared it for racing. With Vasek as the entrant, Jerry Titus took the car to the SCCA D-Production National Championship. This was the start of Vasek's career as a car owner and entrant. Then Davey Jordan won the 1967 Pacific Coast Championship driving a Porsche for Vasek.

Working his magic with Porsches, Vasek campaigned a 917 from 1971 through 1974, entering 934 and 935 models in the Trans-Am. He was a major force in both the Can-Am and Trans-Am, with George Follmer, Hurley Haywood, Jackie Ickx, Jack McAfee, Davey Jordan, Milt Minter, John Morton, Danny Ongais, Sam Posey, Brian Redman and Jody Scheckter driving for him at one time or another. George Follmer won the 1976 Trans-Am championship driving a 935 for Vasek, and Brian Redman scored a second overall in one of the heat races at the 1973 Riverside Can-Am in a 917/10.

After 16 years of constant and untiring effort, Vasek was finally able to bring his family to the United States. Von Neumann helped with the arrangements, even making trips to Prague. After they arrived, however, Vasek and Jindriska became estranged and eventually divorced.

For quite a few years, Johnny Von Neumann, Vasek Polak and I had second homes in Palm Springs. All three of us were on the same street within walking distance of one another. So it was natural that we would get together now and then.

During the 1984 Thanksgiving holiday, we were gathered at Vasek's celebrating with wine and telling tall stories about races we used to have in Palm Springs during the fifties. Having imbibed way too much wine, I mumbled, "Why don't we do it again?" Vasek thought it was a great idea; Johnny just said, "Harrumph." With more enthusiasm than sense, the next day Vasek and I drove all around looking to see if there was a possible location for a course. In those days, the city wasn't nearly as built up as it is now. The result was that we put together an event held on the 1985 Thanksgiving weekend that *Road & Track*'s article speculated "may turn out to be the most successful vintage car race ever held on this continent."

During a reunion race, Dan Gurney in a borrowed Porsche tried to pass both Stirling Moss and Phil Hill on a turn that had room for only two. The result was a severely damaged Speedster. The person from whom I had borrowed the car was, to put it mildly, distraught. Vasek stepped up and restored the Porsche with no cost to Dan or me, to a condition better than it had been prior to the mishap. The owner was mollified, and I was off the hook.

On Sunday, Race Seven was for older sports cars. The cars were due to line up at pre-grid, but an official hustled me over to their paddock. All of the drivers were suited up but sitting on the concrete beside their cars. Vasek Polak had entered a car as a 1937 BMW 328 for John Von Neumann to drive. When I got there, I was told that the entrants wouldn't compete against a replica and that the BMW was, in fact, a replica. I talked with Vasek about it and he admitted it was a replica, But, he said, "It's an *exact* replica." I had to pull the car and the drivers climbed into their cars. Not realizing the rules of vintage racing, Vasek was angry with me for the rest of the day, but after that, all was well.

In 1985, Vasek married Anna Maria Littlejohn, a Czech immigrant and the widow of an American pilot. Our two families often socialized together. I know Vasek was devoted to Anna. In 1993, she died from breast cancer. Vasek contributed $2 million in honor of Anna to the Torrance Memorial Hospital for the establishment of a breast cancer treatment center. Some time later, my wife tried to persuade Vasek to have a date with a single Czech lady doctor she knew, but Vasek refused. I don't think he ever got over Anna's death.

In 1994, we celebrated Vasek's 80th birthday at my home in Palm Springs. He was always my backup whenever we had a party there. If we ran out of booze, his house was right across the street and he usually had cases on hand.

Top: **Vasek and his wife, Anna Maria. Vasek Polak collection.** *Bottom:* **Vasek at his home in Palm Springs in 1990. Photograph by the author.**

By 1995, the Vasek Polak dealerships in Hermosa and Manhattan Beach included Audi, BMW, Saab, Subaru, Volvo and VW, grossing over $50 million a year in sales. His business was the largest taxpayer in the City of Hermosa Beach. Vasek and I often had lunch together at our favorite fish restaurant near his office at the Porsche dealership.

Vasek was not a large man, but he had a very large desk in his office, always piled so high with papers that he could hardly be seen. One day I said, "Hey, Vasek, you have more money than you will ever spend; why don't you sell out, retire and take it easy?" Whereupon he got up, spread his arms wide and remarked, "Look what I have created!"

After Czechoslovakia was freed from Russia, Vasek would often visit there, where he still

Vasek in his Polak Porsche dealership in Hermosa Beach, California, 1995. Vasek Polak collection.

had some family. On March 11, 1997, while driving a new 911 Turbo S on the autobahn on his way back to Germany from Prague, he lost control and had an accident that resulted in severe injuries. He was treated in a hospital in Regensburg, but after a month, he insisted on being taken home to Torrance Memorial. The hospital sent a Learjet with the cabin converted into an intensive-care ward, plus doctors and nurses aboard to fetch him. On April 17, 1997, he suffered cardiac arrest during a fuel stop at Great Falls, Montana. In spite of heroic efforts by the onboard Torrance Memorial doctors, he couldn't be revived.

On April 23, there was a private funeral in Redondo Beach and then, on May 3, a memorial service. The more than 200 in attendance included Porsche executives and members of the Porsche family who had come from Germany. In addition, mutual friends Max Balchowsky, Steve Earle, Davey and Norma Jordan, Milt Minter, John Morton, Scooter Patrick, Jack McAfee, John Von Neumann and Brian Redman were there, plus a host of others.

In addition to his many dealerships and extensive real estate holdings, Vasek left a large and very valuable car collection. The day after the service, Brian and I had a

The Polak Imaging Center at Torrance Memorial Hospital, 1994. Vasek Polak collection.

meeting with Carl Thompson, who took care of the collection. We discussed the best strategy so the cars could be sold for the best prices.

The majority of his fortune went to the Vasek and Anna Maria Polak Charitable Foundation. In the summer of 2008, the foundation established the Polak Imaging Center at the Torrance Memorial Hospital and the Vasek Polak Health Clinic to meet the needs of under- and uninsured workers in the South Bay area of Southern California. The foundation also supports the Vasek Polak Cardiovascular Institute at the Little Company of Mary Hospital in Torrance, a suburb of Los Angeles.

I still miss Vasek sorely and think of him often with fondness.

11

Bill Pollack

Bill Pollack was one of the pioneers of the Southern California sports car scene. His first race was in an MG at the 1950 Palm Springs event, but he is perhaps best known as the winning pilot of Tom Carstens' Allard.

William Mellette Pollack was born on July 7, 1925, in New York City. Bill's younger brother, Jim, was born in 1927. Their parents were in show business; the father was a famous composer and his mother a vaudeville performer. When Bill was 12, the family moved to Los Angeles where he attended Van Nuys High School. The school was also attended by Marilyn Monroe, Jane Russell, Robert Redford and Natalie Wood.

Bill volunteered for the Army in 1943 at age 18 and was assigned to the Army Air Corps. He said that "flight training was more fun than any kid should have." He soloed in a PT-19 in primary training at Sikeston, Missouri. Next, he flew BT-13s and 14s in training at Independence, Kansas. Afterwards, he was sent to Lubbock, Texas, for training at the twin-engine advanced school. After completing training in 1944, he got his wings and was commissioned as a second lieutenant. Lt. Pollack was assigned to the Training Command at Laughlin Field, Texas, where he flew B-24, B-26 and B-29 bombers. Flying cross-country, he landed at the Grand Central Airport in Glendale, California. (In 1955 Bill raced in a sports car road race at this location.) His entire flight crew was from Southern California, so it was a visit home. When the war ended in Europe, he started flying a B-29, our largest bomber. He was likely going to be sent over to bomb Japan, but then the atomic bombs fell; the Japanese surrendered, and Bill was discharged.

Bill came home to California and went to Loyola University on the G.I. Bill. He graduated with a Bachelor of Arts degree. Then he went on to Southwestern University for a degree in law. One day while at Southwestern, he drove by a dealership and saw a red MGTC among other foreign cars. Bill said, "After seeing those cars, all I could think about was me owning an MG."

On Bill's next birthday, his wife, Bobbi, suggested they buy an MG. They found a used TC advertised in the *Los Angeles Times* classifieds. Thus began Bill's lifelong romance with sports cars. He joined the California Sports Car Club and got active in its events. An early one was called the Cento Miglia. It was an illegal race run in the

Newhall area on the outskirts of Los Angeles. Some of the others Bill remembered participating were John Von Neumann, Phil Hill, Roger Barlow and Jack Early. It was called "Cento" because the course was roughly 100 miles (as opposed to "Mille," the famous 1,000-mile race in Italy). John Von Neumann's wife, Elinor, would flag each car off, one at a time, and then she would drive to the end point, Tip's Restaurant in Castaic, where she would time them in. Interestingly enough, Tip's was also a hangout for the local fuzz. On October 25, 2003, Bill re-created the Cento Miglia, leading a band of enthusiasts around the course in his Porsche 911. Sadly, Elinor had died and wasn't there to do the timing.

Bill Pollack was commissioned second lieutenant in the U.S. Army in Lubbock, Texas, 1944.

In 1949, the Cal Club staged a time trial at Goleta, a suburb of Santa Barbara, at an abandoned Marine Corps Base that would later become the Santa Barbara Airport. Bill entered his TC, along with his brother, Jim, who had also acquired a TC, among a flock of other MGs. Phil Hill was there too in his TC.

The April 16, 1950, Palm Springs was the first road race organized by the just incorporated California Sports Car Club and the first post–World War II road race in Southern California. Bill entered his TC, now fitted with a supercharger. The first event was for novices, and it was Bill's first race. He ran it and ended up winning. His win allowed him to run in the 40-lap main event. As Bill remembered,

> My TC was running great and I was hanging in there in third. Sterling Edwards in his special was leading with E. Forbes "Robbie" Robinson second in his MGTD. Then my engine quit. Fortunately, this happened right next to the pits. I pulled over and Ernie McAfee ran up with a large bolt. "I think you need this," he said, "it holds the SU to the blower (supercharger)." Ernie had seen the bolt fall out and picked it up, burning his hand in the process. Running to his pit, he came back with a crescent wrench and refastened the carburetor.

A lap down by then, Bill set off in pursuit. After a time, he was close behind Edwards and Robinson, who were running together. Just as Bill was moving out to try to pass both, the checkered flag dropped and he ended up third. Impressed with Bill's ability, Ernie arranged a ride in John Edgar's MG Special. The next race was held on June 25, 1950, in Santa Ana at an old Army blimp base. This time, Bill was able to finish

Opposite, top: Bill Pollack's brother, Jim (at left), with Bill at Palm Springs on April 16, 1950. *Bottom:* Bill Pollack, driving Tom Carstens' Cadillac-Allard, won the second Pebble Beach Road Race on May 27, 1951. Photograph by Jim Pollack.

second to Edwards. Next on the agenda was the first Pebble Beach on November 5. But the Edgar car had mechanical problems and didn't finish. Afterwards, Jack McAfee inherited the ride in "good old number 88."

From MGs, Bill went to Tom Carstens' J2 Allard. His most memorable rides were two first-place finishes at Pebble Beach in 1951 and 1952. Bill remembered practicing in the J2 on famous California Highway One with 350-pound actor Bobby Coogan riding shotgun.

He also was first overall in the Allard at the 1952 Golden Gate. Bill remembered Golden Gate for me in my book *Golden Gate Remembered*. San Francisco's Golden Gate Park is huge and contains many special features, like the Conservatory, a glass structure modeled after Versailles, given to the City in the early 1900s and a veritable museum of rare botanical species. There are all sorts of wonderful curving roads that sweep through the park.

> The course that was laid out was just over three miles long. I remember that it was particularly fast except for the one hairpin turn at the buffalo enclosure. I don't know if buffalo eat people, but a couple of hay bales and some two-by-twelves were all that stood between the cars and a bunch of bison.

Bill Pollack driving the Baldwin Special at Palm Springs on March 27, 1955. Photograph by Jim Pollack.

The Cad-Allard was running particularly good and, as usual, my competition was Phil Hill, now in his 212 Barchetta 2.6-liter Ferrari. This was one of those courses that really suited my chassis and I found myself drifting through corners with ease. There was one section of the course with three or four curves that was one constant drift through the entire section. You set up for this section and then, if you did it right, everything just sort of fell into place.

Phil and I had a pretty good go until he lost one of his magnetos and the Ferrari engine became a sick six. Even though the Barchetta had a much smaller engine than the Allard, it was a very light car with huge brakes and great handling. I was sorry when the Ferrari dropped back, as we were having such a good time. The race was only run a few more times before the environmentalists determined that the buffalo and the scarlet tanagers were becoming agitated. I'm not sure if we did as much damage to the environment as the boom boxes I heard on a recent visit.

Bill and the Allard ended up winning seven main events.

In 1985 when I staged a vintage revival of Palm Springs, I got Bill a ride in an Allard. Unfortunately, the car was fitted with an automatic transmission, so he wasn't all that happy with it. Bill was reunited with the Carstens J2 Allard at the 1990 Monterey Historics at Laguna Seca. Steve Earle had selected Allard as the featured marque that

On November 9, 1958, Bill drove a Lister-Jaguar at the then new course at Laguna Seca. Photograph by Jim Pollack.

Bill drove a Corvette on November 18, 1956, at Paramount Ranch. He went off the road when his engine failed and he didn't finish. Photograph by Jim Pollack.

year. The car had been restored and had its original number—14—and original colors plus whitewall tires. This was the first time since 1958 that Bill had raced. (The Palm Springs revival was an exhibition.)

After the Allard, Bill drove a plethora of different cars, including Porsches, Jaguars, a Lister, a Morgan and the Baldwin Special. In 1956, he drove the then new Alfa Giulietta Spyder for the importer Max Hoffman on the West Coast, while Carroll Shelby did the same in the East. Bill ran the car ten times that year; his best finishes were firsts at Santa Barbara and Bakersfield.

Bill was a factory driver in a Corvette in 1956. He was second at Bakersfield, fifth at Pomona and first at Buchanan Field. His most memorable ride, however, was the November 18 Paramount Ranch. Bill remembered it for my book *Paramount Ranch Remembered*.

> Paramount Ranch had a unique feature. The straight went over a bridge and then ended in a 270-degree turn. The road then turned around and went under the bridge. This was mighty exciting, and it was fun too. The short tunnel under the bridge was a particular challenge. As

you were coming out of a corner in a drift, you had to get straight for the underpass. There was no room for error.

During practice on Saturday, I was doing fine until one time when I came around that 270-degree turn that took it under the bridge. My throttle stuck wide open. I had just come out of the turn, so I had put my foot all the way in it. On the other side of the bridge I backed off, but nothing happened. The car was still charging ahead. I jumped on the brake pedal and, of course, the engine overpowered the brakes. I had the brakes all locked up and the car slid off the course to the left. I went down an embankment and the car finally came to a stop.

The jolting as I went down the embankment knocked out my wind. A course marshal came rushing over, reached in and shut off the engine, which was screaming. He asked me if I was okay. But I couldn't talk because I couldn't get my breath. All I could get out was "Ah, ah, ah." So he immediately figured I was hurt, having a heart attack or something. So he yelled, "He's hurt, he's hurt!" Before I could say anything, they had me strapped to a gurney, ran me up the hill and slammed me into the ambulance.

The ambulance driver was a full nut case. We started down Cornell Road, which has sweeping turns and many twists. This driver was trying to show me that he was a hero race car driver. I was in the back of the ambulance and he was telling me all these stories and all the while glancing back at me rather than keeping his eyes on the road. It was an unbelievable ride, I'll tell you. I was lucky to get to Northridge Emergency in one piece.

Often those who manage clubs are not drivers. Their forte is being officious. But Bill was an exception and never was, in fact, officious. He served three terms as the president of the California Sports Car Club and was the chair of the Contest Board. Also, he was the non-chairman of a non-organization, the Fabulous Fifties, composed of those who were there then, their descendants and those who wished they were. It is a "non" because it's not incorporated, not a limited anything or otherwise legally recognized. Bill headed it for quite a few years. I was the non-secretary, and we worked together for many years.

Even though he was educated to be an attorney, Bill never practiced. He was always more interested in marketing and sales opportunities. When he was the marketing director for Merle Norman Cosmetics, the company went from $6 million to $30 million gross. He founded a hair care company, created a management-consulting firm and was a licensed commodity broker.

Not content to retire completely, Bill started a late-life writing career. His first book was a novel about a whale, *Tananger*, published in 2001. Next, Bill wrote a book about his racing experiences titled *Red Wheels and White Sidewalls: Confessions of an Allard Racer*. Bill and his wife, Bobbi, had two daughters, Mellette and Leslie,

I took this photograph of Bill in 1986 at the Laguna Seca racetrack. Bill didn't like it, but his wife, Bobbi, liked it very much.

plus two grandchildren. Sadly, Bobbi died on March 24, 2008. They had been married for more than 50 years. Bill's brother, Jim, also raced a few times, but his forte was as a photographer, and a very talented one at that. Jim died in 2004.

Bill skied—both on snow and water—and enjoyed progressive jazz. He kept fit playing golf and riding his bicycle. I also enjoy bike riding and went on a few jaunts with Bill. He had ten years on me and I had to work hard to keep up.

A highlight of Bill's last year was a celebration of his 92nd birthday on July 7, 2017, at his home attended by quite a number of his family.

Bill passed away peacefully at his home on July 16, 2017, at age 92 with his daughter Mellette at his side.

12

Carroll Shelby

Interestingly enough, Carroll Shelby's life more or less divided itself into decades. The forties were World War II and his Army Air Corps time followed by the fifties and racing. In the sixties came the Cobras, the Shelby Mustangs, and the Ford GTs. The seventies were his Africa years and the eighties the Dodge time. The nineties saw a revival of Cobras and Mustangs, and in the new millennium, he developed his various enterprises into what amounts to a mini-conglomerate. Carroll himself had become a true icon.

Carroll Hall Shelby was born on January 11, 1923, in Leesburg, Texas. Leesburg is a small town 120 miles northeast of Dallas with a population of about 200. His dad was a rural mail carrier. Shel's earliest remembrance was his dad delivering mail in a horse-drawn buggy in which, on occasion, he accompanied his father. He had only one sibling, a sister, Ann.

According to Shel, "In high school my consuming interest was automobiles and airplanes, unfortunately not subjects on the curriculum." He got a part-time job sweeping out hangars at the local airport. Also, his father took him to dirt-track ovals to see racing. Shel's education never went beyond high school.

After the Japanese attacked Pearl Harbor in 1941, Shel joined the Army. He was 18. One time he told me the story, and I wrote it all down. So I'll let him tell about his war years in his own words:

> The first thing they did with me when I joined the Army Air Corps was to put me on a train with 75 other recruits and shipped us out to Randolph Field, Texas. We arrived about five o'clock in the afternoon in the middle of a downpour, and they shoved us into some tents that were far from dry. Next morning, we were awakened at five o'clock with our mess kits and given breakfast. Then they gave us mops and told us to go to work in the hangar. Basic training had begun.
>
> When basic finally came to an end, I assumed that we would be assigned as aircraft mechanics or at least be given something to do with aircraft. Instead, I was assigned to a detail hauling chicken manure from an old abandoned chicken farm to various flowerbeds around Randolph Field. This detail continued for three months!
>
> Then they passed a new regulation that those of us in the Air Corps who had finished high school and were anxious to get into flying could become flying sergeants. There was a minimum weight limit for fellows of a certain height and I happened to be about 10 pounds under

the requirement. I had no alternative but to stuff myself with bananas and milk and suffer for three hours until I could get pumped out after the physical.

Anyway, I made it in November 1942 and was sent off to a course of preflight training at Lackland Army Air Force Base in San Antonio, Texas. Next, I took my basic flight training at Sherman, Texas. I courted my girlfriend, Jeanne, more by airplane than any other way! She lived on a farm near Dallas and I used to fly over and throw her notes in my flying boots. I would fly out low over Jeanne's house and drop the boot right in her yard.

Shelby and Jeanne Fields were married on December 18, 1944. Shelby family collection.

Around September 1943, they made me a flying sergeant and in December of that same year I was commissioned a second lieutenant. As it turned out, I never rose any higher nor did I try for a further promotion. I was more interested in flying and having fun in those days. I loved to fly, but I never did take to military discipline.

I finished twin-engine training at Ellington Field in Houston, Texas, and after that started flying bombardiers. My usual ship was a twin-engine Beechcraft AT-11 with an occasional B-18 thrown in. Then I moved on to another bombardier school and flew B-25s and 26s, finally ending up in a B-29 at Denver, Colorado.

I got out of the service in 1945. I had been in the Army four years and six months and had never left the country except to fly out over the Gulf of Mexico. I never did any operational flying but instead—acting as an instructor—flew students and also took the job of test pilot. Sure, I would have liked to fly combat. (At that time, the Army kept the very best pilots in the U.S. to train new pilots.)

When I made a formal request for my discharge, a courteous major received me with an ingratiating smile. "Wouldn't you sooner switch to the Reserve?" he inquired. "It offers many benefits plus the fact you can continue to keep up your flying." "Negative, sir," I told him. "Just let me get out altogether." "As you wish," the major said and sighed. I saluted and walked out and that was the last I saw of the Army Air Corps.

After mustering out in 1945, Shel tried a number of businesses including chicken ranching. Unfortunately, all the chickens died of Limberneck disease. Then, he got interested in cars and racing. Again, I'll let Carroll tell about it in his own words:

> Ed Wilkins and I used to go to the dirt track races along with my father in the old days. We also shared an interest in airplanes and automobiles at a very young age. At this time Ed had a couple of cars, one of which he built himself. The other was an MGTC. The homebuilt

special, which so far as I recall didn't have a name, interested me quite a bit. It featured a ladder-type frame of quite a modern concept, 1932 Ford V8 suspension including a solid front axle, a flathead Ford engine and a homemade body similar to those you see on fifties-era sports car specials. Still, it was a nice job, well put together and reflected a lot of work and time. I told Ed so and suddenly, he turned to me with a straight face and asked, "Would you like to drive the thing for me?" "Drive it?" I said, "Where?" "There's a drag race in a few days [this was in January 1952] at the Grand Prairie Naval Station between Dallas and Fort Worth." "You mean just straight dragging on a strip?" "Yeah," he nodded. "It's a quarter mile and I'd sure like to see how this baby goes." "You just got yourself a driver," I laughed.

As things turned out, there wasn't much to it. My opposition consisted mainly of a bunch of sports cars—nearly all MGs—and I just ran away and hid from them. When you consider what I had under the hood, it was not exactly surprising, but the nice thing was that Ed's special handled just fine and did nothing unpredictable.

It seemed to me that Ed got a charge all out of proportion to what I had done, but then he had built the car himself and worked all those Ford bits into the design and came up with something that actually ran pretty well. So I guess he was entitled to feel happy.

Shelby in his dress uniform, 1944. Shelby family collection.

After my experience driving Ed Wilkins's special in the drag race, one day he said to me, "I think you've got the touch, Shel. Would you like to have a go in my TC in a real sports car race? I mean one with corners and all that."

"Why not," I replied. "Then we might as well start preparing the car without delay," he said. "There's some races around here in May."

"Okay," I replied. "But what's this bit about preparing? We're not equipped to do any serious work on your MG other than just check out to see everything's tight, the timing is right, the plugs gapped properly and so forth," I said. "That's just what I meant," Ed assured me. "No modification; just a routine check out."

We did just that. In those days, since I wasn't working regularly but just making out on a little of this and a little of that—odd jobs and buying and selling bits and pieces—time wasn't of any real importance.

The first race we entered was held on a small airport near Caddo Mills, Texas. Quite a crowd turned out to watch, because it was one of the early Sports Car Club of America races. The course was laid out close to this little town about 40 miles from Dallas on U.S. 30. It was a one-day affair on May 3, 1952. As far as Ed's car was concerned, it was really as stock as the day it had left the factory. The windshield was on, the spare tire and the whole bit. I remember I wore a helmet, but I haven't any idea what number our car carried on its side. I can't remember much about the race itself except that I won.

Next, we went all the way to Norman, Oklahoma, the home of the University of Oklahoma. The course turned out to be triangular and easy to drive, even though it was one of the first stabs taken in the Southwest at a real road circuit. What we ran on was actually a huge concrete and gravel airplane parking area that had not been used since the war. Someone had dreamed up the idea of using three pylons to mark each of the angles of the triangle. Each lap was about a mile or a mile and a half, I'm not sure which, but enough to work up a little bit of speed.

The first race, as I recall, was for MGs only. I don't think I had a very good starting position. I was somewhere in the middle of a pack of 15 or 20 identical automobiles, I remember watching for the flag to start dropping. Then I let out the clutch, pushed the throttle down and squeezed through a series of gaps by no more than the thickness of the paint. This didn't put me in the lead by any means, but at least it gained me a few places to make up for that lousy spot on the grid.

One guy in a car that looked exactly like Ed's drove a pretty good race and gave me a lot more trouble than I had expected for a couple of laps. I just waited for him to make a mistake and let his tail end come around a bit too much. Under the pressure of pursuit, he did just that. It's never much fun having someone breathing down your exhaust pipe because you don't really know whether they're fully extended or playing a cat-and-mouse game. The pursuing driver has a much easier time of it. I finally got by him and into the lead.

Well, I won that one by a good margin with the rest of the field strung out. Ed Wilkins was tickled pink at having his car win. When they started lining up a bunch of XK120 Jaguars for the next event, an official came over and asked if we'd like to run the MG since I had won the previous race.

Ed jumped at the offer. Then he turned to me a bit sheepishly and asked, "Think you can make it Shel? I mean, you don't have to go with those Jags unless you want to, you know."

"What can we lose," I replied, "besides some tire tread? Sure, I'll run." I don't have to remind anyone, even today, that an XK120 was an entirely different breed of cat from an MGTC. But back of my mind was an idea—maybe something I'd read or seen someplace—that those Jags didn't corner half as well as a lot of people were led to believe. They had a thing called understeer where, when you try to take a corner really fast and the corner is sharp enough, the front end starts to wash out on you. But against this they had tremendous speed and about twice as much acceleration as the little TC. It didn't take me long to figure out that if I was going to skunk those XKs, I had better do it on the turns and not wait for them to gobble me up along the straights. Pretty soon I worked out a pattern of going wide at full bore in a kind of drift that converted the triangle into a rough circle. I had to use the full width of the runway and the pylons ceased to have any meaning, except as rough guides, but this idea paid off. I got the checker after a very enjoyable drive that taught me several useful things.

Not to take anything away from the opposition, I guess I must have had a little bit of ability or something and didn't recognize it at the time, because I don't mind admitting that no one was more surprised than Carroll Shelby when I beat those Jags. The next race was back to Caddo Mills again on July 2, but the MG engine crapped out on me and I didn't finish.

The next race I entered was in August 1952 at a place called Okmulgee, Oklahoma, a county seat about 25 miles south of Tulsa. That time, I drove an XK120 and beat a bunch of other Jaguars to win without too much trouble.

Before the Okmulgee race, a Louisiana sportsman, Charles Brown, had asked me if I'd drive his Cad-Allard for him and I had agreed to do this. In those days, the Cad-Allard was a mighty powerful beast with a lot of pep, even though it owned the craziest front end you ever did see on a racing automobile; so I guess my being asked to drive this baby could be taken as a compliment.

I drove Brown's well-prepared Allard for the first time at Caddo Mills in November 1952 and again at the same venue in January 1953. The November event, by the way, also happened to be the very first race that Masten Gregory ever drove in, and I must say he had an awful lot of guts, cutting his teeth as a race driver in a Cadillac-powered Allard.

For that time, there seemed to be quite an array of powerful and expensive machinery. Masten gave me a good battle and would have finished second, but unfortunately his throttle linkage broke. It was a funny thing; I think Masten and I had less experience in driving hairy stuff like the Allards than any of the other drivers. Yet somehow, I ended up winning and, as I say, Masten lost second through no fault of his own. Driving a brute like an Allard for the first time in a race, you had to feel your way a bit carefully at first. It was rather like walking across a floor strewn with marbles.

When Christmas came around and the end of 1952, I had run a number of races and won some, collecting a few little trophies at the same time. In those days, it was unthinkable for a gentleman to accept any money for his racing, and sure enough, I didn't earn myself a cent. Only the boys at Indy or a stock car or midget driver would soil his hands with money in this noble sport. At least, that was the popular misconception of the times.

Until later in the decade, almost all road races in the United States were run by the Sports Car Club of America. In order to race, a driver had to belong to the club and be licensed by it. The rules at that time were if a driver accepted money to race, he or she was suspended and not allowed to race in an SCCA-sanctioned event for one year. The rule, however, didn't apply to events held outside the United States. Some drivers—notably John Fitch and Shel himself—accepted money to race in other countries while, at the same time, maintaining their amateur status with the SCCA.

But in actuality, while no prize money was paid at these early SCCA races, some drivers did, in fact, receive payment for their services. In those days, there were a number of wealthy "sportsmen" who owned fast and expensive cars and wanted to see them win races. Talented drivers like Shel were employed to compete. The amounts paid were, of course, not a matter of public record except to the IRS. Among those sportsmen were Allen Guiberson, Tony Parravano, John Edgar, Temple Buell and the Camoradi Team, all of whom employed Shel, among others, at one time or another.

Two-time Indy winner and national champion Rodger Ward told a story about Shel. Ward observed that Shel was a fair country driver and that if he were to turn pro and compete on the IndyCar circuit, he would make some considerable money. Shel asked Ward how much he might expect. After Rodger told him an approximate amount, Carroll replied that he couldn't afford it. He was making more than that driving as an "amateur."

He borrowed an XK120 from a friend and won again at Okmulgee, Oklahoma. Later that year in his third race, he drove Roy Cherryholmes's Cadillac-Allard to first place at an SCCA event at Caddo Mills, Texas.

Other successes followed in the Allard, culminating with a good finish at the January 1954 Grand Prix of Argentina.

While there, Aston Martin team manager John Wyer noticed Shel's talent and offered him a drive at the 1954 12 Hours of Sebring in a DB3S. Shel and his co-driver, Charlie Wallace, were among the front-runners when the rear axle broke on the 77th lap. Wyer asked Shel to come to England and become a team member. His first event was at Aintree, where he placed second behind Duncan Hamilton in a C-Type Jaguar. Next, Wyer teamed Shel up with Paul Frere for Le Mans. At 1:50 in the morning, they had to retire because of a broken spindle. In August, he started driving for Donald Healey and helped set new Class D records at Bonneville in a production Austin-Healey. At Mexico in November, Shel flipped his Austin-Healey and suffered serious injuries that might have very well put a lesser man out of racing.

For the most part, Carroll Shelby drove for John Edgar during both 1956 and 1957 in a Ferrari. This photograph was taken at Torrey Pines in 1956. Shelby family collection.

At the March 1955 Sebring—with his arm in a cast and his broken hand taped to the steering wheel—Shel teamed with Phil Hill in Allen Guiberson's three-liter Monza Ferrari. At first, the pair were scored overall winners, but because of a protest, found themselves officially in second. Shel continued with Guiberson and took an overall win at Torrey Pines in July, lapping the entire field. I met Shel that year at the Torrey Pines race. Later, we would become very close friends. For the rest of the year, he drove for Tony Parravano in Europe.

Back in the United States in 1956, Shel won just about everything there was to win. Entered in a total of 17 events by various car owners, Shel won 13 of them. At the Cuban Grand Prix in Edgar's 4.9 Ferrari, he was second behind World Champion Juan Fangio in a 3-liter Maserati.

At the conclusion of the U.S. season, he was crowned the SCCA National Champion and the *Sports Illustrated* Sports Car Driver of the Year. The next year the same magazine gave him the title Driver of the Year. Through the end of the decade, success followed success, culminating in winning the 1959 24 Hours of Le Mans in an Aston Martin.

On June 21, 1959, Shelby won the ultimate in road racing, Le Mans. Shelby family collection.

In 1958, he had started competing in Formula One, but in February 1960 he started to experience chest pains. Even so, that year he won the USAC Driving Championship, but then angina pectoris forced him to retire. One of the most successful road racing careers by an American was merely a prelude to even more spectacular achievements.

Even though successful as a driver, Carroll Shelby had long been interested in creating his own sports car. His criteria were that it had to be a real performer yet driver friendly on the highway while at the same time being relatively inexpensive in comparison to Ferraris, Maseratis, Aston Martins and the like.

His first opportunity came in 1959. At that time, Shel and Jim Hall were partners in their Dallas dealership as well as in the import of Listers. Their friend, fellow Texan Gary Laughlin, got the idea of putting an Italian body on Corvettes. Laughlin persuaded Chevrolet division manager Ed Cole to sell them three stock Corvette chassis complete with 283-CID fuel-injected engines and transmissions. They were shipped to Italy where the Carrozzeria Scaglietti design team created handmade aluminum coupe bodies, which turned out to be 400 pounds lighter than a 1959 Corvette.

The concept was for the Shelby-Hall partnership to handle the export-import and marketing. But as it turned out, the cars were so good that General Motors backed out and declined to sell any more chassis, so the idea had to be abandoned. Each of the three ended up with a car. Shelby's is now owned by the Petersen Automotive Museum. Undoubtedly the experience provided Shel with food for thought.

After his retirement from racing, Shel's first venture was the creation of the Shelby School of High Performance Driving, which opened in 1961. He made an arrangement to rent Riverside Raceway during weekdays. The idea was to teach one student at a time for a week. Shel hired Pete Brock to manage the school as well as provide much of the instruction. Such was Shel's fame that a single $90 ad brought 1,400 replies. John Timanus later joined Brock and Shel as teachers.

At the same time, Shel had obtained distributorships for Goodyear racing tires and Champion spark plugs. He operated in a small office and space rented from Dean Moon's shop in Santa Fe Springs, California.

A successful sports car of the time was the British AC, which sported a two-liter engine based on the famous pre-war BMW. In 1961, the manufacturer of the engine—the Bristol Aeroplane Company, which had obtained the rights to the design from Germany in war reparations—decided to stop producing the engines. This put AC in a bind, and Shel heard about it. So in September, he sent a letter proposing that AC produce rollers and ship them to him in the United States for the installation of a small-block American V8.

Initially, Shel had the venerable Chevrolet engine in mind, but then he heard that Ford had developed a new casting process that let them make a lightweight V8 at a low cost. Meanwhile, Charles Hurlock at AC wrote back that he would be interested if a suitable engine would be available. Whereupon Shel got in touch with Dave Evans at Ford. Evans sent Shel two of the new engines, which arrived at Santa Fe Springs in November 1961.

In February 1962, the first AC roller arrived at Shel's Santa Fe Springs shop at the Moon facility. In only one day, Shel and Dean Moon installed a Ford 260-CID engine and a Borg-Warner four-speed transmission. The two friends test-drove the car—which Shel named a Cobra—that same day.

Meanwhile, Lance Reventlow had decided to wind up his Scarab project. The facility, located in Venice, California, became available, so Shelby moved his operation and took over Lance's Princeton Drive shop in March 1962. The new business was named Shelby American and Ray Geddes from Ford came on board to coordinate. One of his first duties was to keep Ford's involvement at a low profile from concerns regarding liability. The first production Cobra—CSX 2000—was completed in April and shipped to the New York Auto Show where it was placed in the Ford display. As a result, Ford dealers began to place orders along with deposits. The second car—CSX 2001—was shipped from AC in England to Ed Hugus, who had a large dealership in Pittsburgh, where the engine, transmission and rear end were installed. Shelby appointed Ed, a close friend and successful race driver, as his first dealer and later as distributor for the eastern states.

Production started in Venice, but it was slow because extensive alterations on the AC chassis were required. Nevertheless, in August 1962, papers were submitted to the FIA for homologation in the over-two-liter class. Acceptance by the FIA meant that

Cobras would be allowed to compete with other production cars. The FIA requirement, however, was that at least 100 cars had to be completed within 12 months. The FIA ended up approving the application even though only eight had been completed by then.

On October 13, 1962, a Cobra was entered by Shelby American in the Los Angeles Times Grand Prix at Riverside. Shel selected Inglewood, California, Honda dealer Bill Krause to drive in the three-hour enduro for production cars that preceded the main event. The race was not only the first ever for a Cobra but also the debut of the new Sting Ray Corvette. At the start, Dave MacDonald in a Sting Ray led off followed by Krause. But Dave went out early on with mechanical problems, allowing Krause to take over. Bill led for the first half hour, but then the new Cobra broke an axle. Doug Hooper inherited the lead and won in another Sting Ray. Afterwards, Shelby remarked, "It was a tough break, but at least a consolation to know we were in front when the axle broke."

By November, the Shelby American Cobra production line had been worked out to produce one car a day. Similar operations were set up by Hugus in Pittsburgh as well as in Providence, Rhode Island.

Meanwhile, another British car manufacturer took notice of the Cobra: the Rootes Group, which was making the Sunbeam Alpine, a great but underpowered car. An engineless Alpine was delivered to Shelby American with an order to install a small-block Ford. At the same time, another roller was sent to Ken Miles, who had an independent shop, with the same order. Miles completed the job over a single weekend. It took a little longer at Shelby American, but that one turned out to be the first Sunbeam Tiger.

Shortly thereafter, Miles went to work for Shelby and became one of the most important Shelby employees. Ken and Dave MacDonald were entered at an SCCA regional race at Riverside on January 2–3, 1963, in Production Class A. Showing the Sting Rays the way home, Miles was first on Saturday (the 2nd), with Dave second. On Sunday, Miles made a pit stop after the first lap, letting MacDonald capture the win. Then, from dead last, Ken passed everyone except Dave to take second. The best Corvette was Dick Guldstrand in third. From then on, Cobras dominated most SCCA events. With similar power, they were some 1,000 pounds lighter than a Corvette.

Shelby's first entry in international competition was in the Daytona 3 Hour Continental on February 17, 1963. Dave MacDonald managed a fourth. At the 12 Hours of Sebring the following month, Miles, Phil Hill and Lew Spencer were eleventh. It should be noted that these events included sports-racing cars with Ferraris and the like dominating.

By June, Shelby American had completed 125 Cobras. Shel wanted to enter Le Mans, but Ford declined to finance the effort. So Shelby put together a deal with AC Cars and Ed Hugus, with each fielding a car. The AC entry finished seventh with only Ferraris ahead. Ed was disqualified for adding oil inside 25 laps. By the end of 1963, a Cobra had won the SCCA A-Production National Championship as well as the U.S. Road Racing Championship.

The Shelby American team in Venice, California, 1963: (from left) Skip Hudson, Ken Miles, Peter Jopp, Lew Spencer, David MacDonald and Carroll Shelby. Shelby collection, courtesy Tracey Smith.

By February 1964, Shelby American had completed the first FIA roadster as well as the first Daytona Coupe. In June, a Daytona Coupe driven by Dan Gurney and Bob Bondurant placed fourth at Le Mans and first in the GT class. In September, the first GT350 Mustangs were completed and the next month the first 427 Cobra. A 289 Cobra again won the SCCA A-Production National Championship.

In 1965 Shelby moved his facility to a location near Los Angeles International Airport, and Ford turned its GT-40 project over to Shel. A GT-40 won Daytona and a Coupe won the GT class. Bondurant and Jo Schlesser took first overall at Sebring. When all the dust settled that year, Shelby had wrestled the FIA World Manufacturers' Championship in the GT category away from Ferrari.

The year 1966 turned out to be the year of Shel's greatest triumphs and deepest tragedy. Ken Miles and Lloyd Ruby won the Daytona Continental and again at Sebring in a GT-40. Miles and Denny Hulme were well on their way to a victory at Le Mans and the so-called triple crown of racing when some unusual pit signals gave the win to Bruce McLaren and Chris Amon in another GT-40. Shel and the GT-40s completely dominated international sports car racing and won the World Manufacturers' Championship. But Shel's close friend Ken Miles was killed testing at Riverside.

Shel won again at Le Mans in 1967. Another highlight that year was Shel's first chili cook-off. But the rest of the decade was a slow decline for Shelby American. The company lost its lease on the LAX facility and moved to Torrance, California. The following year, the last Cobra was sold, and Ford took over production of Shelby Mustangs, moving them to one of its own facilities. In 1969, the Mustang project ended because of declining sales and Shelby American closed its doors. In 1970, Ford ended its racing agreement with Shelby even though a GT-40 had won again at Le Mans the previous year.

The seventies were Shel's Africa years. He spent about nine months of each year there, first in Botswana, then Angola and finally the Central African Republic. In the latter, he made a deal with the government to control hunting rights. He also got involved in diamond trading. Of those years, he remarked, "I didn't make a lot of money, but I had a lot of fun." Back in the United States, he had come out with his Carroll Shelby's Original Texas Chili Mix, which developed into a big business that was eventually sold to Kraft Foods. In addition, in partnership with Al Dowd, an aftermarket specialty wheel company was established.

In 1982, Lee Iacocca, CEO of Chrysler, which had just emerged from bankruptcy and had a reputation for producing rather dowdy cars, persuaded his friend Shel to perform the same magic he had on the Mustang. In 1983, the Dodge Shelby Charger was introduced with the Dodge Omni GLH the following year. Through the decade and until 1993, 17 different models were produced. In 1989, Shelby tried to revive the Can-Am Series by building a spec car with a Chrysler engine. He made 76, but while the idea didn't catch on in the United States, it did in South Africa, where a series was instituted. But during that same time, Shelby's heart condition worsened to the extent that he underwent a transplant in 1990.

Shel also worked on and constructed the first prototype Dodge Viper, a real honest-to-goodness sports car. Shelby was on hand at the 1989 Detroit Automobile Show when it was introduced. He also drove it as the pace car at the 1991 Indianapolis 500 with General Norman Schwarzkopf in the right-hand seat.

In the meantime, used Cobras were receiving more and more cachet, with prices rapidly climbing. As a result, a number of companies started to make replicas, most with fiberglass bodies. Some were sold without engines and classified by departments of motor vehicles as kit cars, not subject to the regulations imposed on new vehicles. Not to be outdone by these interlopers, Shel got the idea of producing a limited

Shelby at the 1986 Monterey Historics. Photograph by the author.

Shelby (left) with Peyton Cramer and one of the first Cobras, Venice, 1962. Shelby collection, courtesy Tracey Smith.

number of "new" 1966 427 S/C Cobras—the so-called Continuation Series—that carried serial numbers he had applied for during the sixties but never used. He made a deal with Mike McCluskey, in a shop near the Torrance, California, airport, to make them.

At the same time, Shel designed a sports car from the ground up that he dubbed the Series 1. It was a high-performance roadster that utilized a 320-bhp Oldsmobile Aurora V8 engine. Production started in 1999 at Shelby American with a total of 248 units made. Some were supercharged and had larger brakes and a heavy-duty clutch. But at the same time, Series 1 cars are user friendly with power steering, power windows and air conditioning. The following year, it appeared that the cost of meeting federal safety standards would be prohibitive, and production ceased.

In 2003, Shelby Automobiles was formed, and production of Shelby Mustangs started at the Las Vegas plant. As was done in the sixties, cars were shipped from Ford to Las Vegas, where they were transformed into Shelby GTs and sold by selected Ford dealers. The Las Vegas facility also includes a museum featuring Shelby collectibles.

During his heart transplant, Shel became aware of the high medical costs for patients, not only for the operation itself but also the care and medications that follow. He established the Carroll Shelby Children's Foundation to provide financial aid. His first recipient was an infant named Leah Smith who needed transplant medication in 1991. She was within days of dying because her parents didn't have the necessary funds. Today, Leah is healthy and an Olympic-level figure skater. Shelby made arrangements for the foundation to continue after his death.

It's mind-boggling to consider all of the things with which Shelby was involved. Carroll Shelby International includes Shelby Automobiles in Las Vegas and another plant in the Los Angeles suburb of Gardena, where licensing is headquartered along with his car collection and the foundation.

Carroll Shelby's energy was astonishing, particularly for someone in his eighties. He had two ranches in Texas, where he grew livestock. He traveled around in two private airplanes, one prop, the other a jet. In addition to the two ranches, he had homes in Los Angeles and Las Vegas.

Shelby was married a number of times. His first was Jeanne Fields. They were married during the war and had three children, Sharon, Patrick and Michael, and were divorced in 1960. In 1997, his sixth wife, Lena Dahl, was killed in a traffic accident. Afterwards, he said that he was never going to get married again. Nevertheless, four months later, he married a charming Englishwoman, Cleo, a former model who drove in European rallies.

On May 10, 2012, Carroll Hall Shelby died after a six-month illness. At the end of November 2011, he was in and out of the hospital quite a number of times. My son, David, would take him. Then when he felt somewhat better, he would ask David to transport him home. This went on until he was so ill he couldn't return home anymore.

About two weeks before he died, his sons, Michael and Patrick, came to the hospital in Los Angeles and took him home to Dallas and put him in the Baylor University Hospital, where he died.

During the months of his hospitalization in Los Angeles, he didn't want anyone to visit him other than David and his wife, Cleo. He didn't want anyone to see him in the condition he was in. Shelby and I talked now and then via his cell phone and I repeatedly told him I wanted to visit.

During our cell phone calls, we talked about a number of things, among them a pictorial odyssey book. He was anxious that I put it together. As it turned out, it took me more than a year after his demise. I wanted to get it right, something Shelby would approve of.

When he passed away at Baylor, he was surrounded by his kids: Sharon, Michael and Patrick. He was also survived by a number of grandchildren and six of his seven wives. His first wife, Jeanne, lived in Dallas along with the three kids. I never met her, but we would talk occasionally on the phone. The last time I called, I was told by her caregiver that she was so ill she couldn't come to the phone. Jeanne died on October 12, 2012. So the children lost both their parents in the same year.

All of my relationships with Shel, which went back many years, were more than cordial. He was always friendly, cooperative and without a huge ego.

The pictorial odyssey book, *Carroll Shelby: A Collection of My Favorite Racing Photos*, was published in 2016. Before that, I had written two other books about him: *Shelby: The Race Driver* and *The Shelby American Story*.

13

John Von Neumann

John von Neumann (1903–1957) is an important name in the history of the second half of the 20th century. A Princeton professor, he was an eminent mathematician and physicist, instrumental in the development of computer science, a participant in the Manhattan Project to develop the atom bomb and a Nobel laureate. (His Jewish father had purchased an Austrian title, hence the von.)

There was, however, another John Von Neumann, who was important to the development of the post–World War II sports car craze, particularly Porsches. We called him Johnny. And, interestingly, the two have more than the same name in common. Both fled Austria when Chancellor Kurt von Schuschnigg turned the country over to Adolf Hitler and both immigrated to the United States.

Our Johnny was one of the three who created the California Sports Car Club, which, in the sixties, was to become the largest region of the SCCA. He was the first to race Porsches on the West Coast and championed Ferraris on the track, both for himself and for some top drivers. From a small foreign-car repair shop, he built an empire that became the largest Porsche-VW distributorship in the United States and was a particular friend of both Ferry Porsche and Enzo Ferrari.

Johnny was born in Vienna in 1921. His father was a distinguished surgeon who treated royalty, including the kings of England and Spain. After the Anschluss, the family fled to Switzerland. In 1939 Dr. Von Neumann, who had been invited to become a lecturer at Columbia University, and the family—including Johnny, his mother and two sisters—moved to New York City. Unfortunately, the doctor died that year.

Johnny enrolled at New York University. An aficionado of musical theater and a stage-door "Johnny," he became enamored with a Ziegfeld Follies dancer—Elinor—whom he later married.

In 1940, Johnny loaded up his Lagonda—purchased with part of his inheritance from his father—and transferred to the University of Southern California.

In 1942, Johnny sold the Lagonda and enlisted in the U.S. Army. He was—serendipitously—sent for basic training at Camp Callan near San Diego where, in the next decade, he would compete in the first sports car race at Torrey Pines, the site of the former Army base.

13. John Von Neumann

Because of his language fluency, Johnny became a member of the fledgling Central Intelligence Agency. In 1944, he participated as an intelligence officer in the invasion of Germany and, after the surrender, was sent to Salzburg, Austria, where he worked in the denazification program.

With the war's end and mustering out, Johnny got a job as a salesman at Roger Barlow's International Motors in Beverly Hills. Interested in competition, Johnny, along with Roger and another employee, Taylor Lucas, formed the California Sports Car Club. Their first event was a time trial held in the hills of Palos Verdes in August 1947. Johnny won in an SS100 Jaguar. After putting on a number of other trial-type events, the club staged its first road race at Palm Springs in April 1950. After blowing the head gasket in his supercharged MG, Johnny borrowed a Riley and competed in the production race. The next month, he won the very first race held through the forest at Pebble Beach in his MG.

Meanwhile, Johnny, along with another enthusiast, wealthy Secondo Guasti, opened a small speed shop they called Competition Motors. Soon they were selling,

John Von Neumann (at left, in his MGTC) ran in one of the first California Sports Car Club races in July 1949. At this time, there were no road courses. The event was at Carrell Speedway, an oval race course near Los Angeles. John Von Neumann collection.

John in his Porsche follows a Simca driven by Louis Van Dyke at Torrey Pines on July 20, 1952. John Von Neumann collection.

as well as modifying and repairing, foreign cars. Johnny acquired one of the first Porsches, cut the top off, then entered and won his event at the 1952 Torrey Pines. That same year, Johnny became a Porsche dealer, and the next year he established a Porsche-VW distributorship. By 1956, the network included 37 dealerships selling almost 10,000 cars a year. His wife, Elinor—somewhat older than John—was also active in managing the business. Johnny was her second husband; the first had been Joe Bigelow, who was Jack Benny's chief writer. Elinor and Joe had a daughter, Josie, who strangely enough, had some facial features similar to Johnny's. He would become irritated when anyone took Josie for his real daughter since she was only a few years younger than he was. (Josie died in March 1997.)

Although Johnny's early racing was at the wheel of MGs, he soon changed to Porsches. Then in 1954, he bought a 500 Mondial Ferrari from Porfirio Rubirosa. When Johnny couldn't beat Ken Miles's MG Special (R-1), he hired Ken to work at Competition Motors, putting Miles in Porsches while Johnny drove Ferraris. One time I asked Johnny if he had kept track of his racing. He replied that he had been in so many races he couldn't remember. (A record was compiled by Michael Lynch and can be found in his book *American Sports Car Racing in the 1950s.*)

13. John Von Neumann

Ken Miles won the Semi-Main Event at Torrey Pines on January 15, 1956. Ken is congratulated by John Von Neumann, who had entered the Porsche Spyder. John was the Porsche distributor for the Western states. John Von Neumann collection.

Even though he was often in the winner's circle, Johnny was conservative behind the wheel and seldom took unwarranted chances. His only accident occurred at March Field in 1954. Johnny had entered a new 550 Porsche Spyder. During Saturday practice as he was coming down the pit straight, an MG pulled out directly in front of him. The Spyder was demolished, but Johnny walked away without a scratch!

Johnny's best year as a race driver was 1957. He had ordered a new 625 TRC Ferrari, and it was shipped from Italy to Mexico for the April Avandaro event, which Johnny won. Five additional overall wins followed that year, as well as numerous class victories.

Others who drove for Von Neumann in addition to Ken included Phil Hill, Richie Ginther, Jack McAfee and his stepdaughter Josie. One time, he even gave a ride at a hill climb to actor John Hart, who was the last Lone Ranger.

On October 20, 1957, John Von Neumann won the Main Event at Riverside. His wife, Elinor, is at his side. John Von Neumann collection.

John Von Neumann won the Main Event on October 27, 1957, at the Pomona Fairgrounds. John Von Neumann collection.

In 1957, he added a Ferrari franchise to his empire—Ferrari Representatives of California—managed by Richie Ginther. In 1959, Johnny and Elinor parted ways. The Ferraris and the Ferrari business went to her in the divorce settlement. Johnny's last year behind the wheel was 1959.

Afterwards, Von Neumann started to spend considerable time in Europe and, in 1965, acquired the Ferrari franchise for the country of Switzerland. In 1973, he sold the Porsche-VW distributorship to the factory, and Johnny joined the ranks of the super wealthy. Next, he turned his enthusiasm for yachting into a suc-

John in his Hollywood office. John Von Neumann collection.

cessful business, and then performed the same financial magic after acquiring a Learjet.

Although we knew one another during the fifties, Johnny and my family became close some years later when we were neighbors in Palm Springs. His house was across the street a few blocks away from mine. Porsche expert and Johnny's close friend Vasek Polak also had a house on the same short street. Vasek and Johnny often enjoyed dirt biking in the area before it became overdeveloped. The last time we saw Johnny was on the occasion of my grandson's christening in January 2003. At the subsequent party at our house, Johnny was the first to arrive and the last to leave.

During those years, Johnny usually wintered in Palm Springs and lived the rest of the time at his chalet on Lake Geneva, his condo in Beverly Hills or his live-aboard yacht—complete with captain, crew and chef—on the Mediterranean. Although he had a young wife—named Monica—we never saw her in Palm Springs. There was, however, a succession of live-in girlfriends there. One was a European model born in Tunisia. One day he asked me to photograph her posing with his latest Ferrari. I gave Johnny the negatives as well as the prints, so I can't reproduce one here.

In the fall of 2003, Johnny suffered a stroke, and he died that Christmas Eve. There was no service of any kind, but eventually Monica scheduled a remembrance gathering at the Petersen Museum. However, she suddenly canceled it without explanation and, I understand, abruptly left for Switzerland.

John with his wife, Monica. Photograph by Ginny Dixon.

I took this portrait of John at his house in Palm Springs in 1969. He wouldn't smile, so I reached over and tickled him. Photograph by the author.

14

Rodger Ward

For the last 20 years or so of his life, Rodger Ward and I were good friends. I had met him once during the fifties when he drove a customer's Devin SS when I was the Devin distributor. Later we became close friends when he drove my car at the 1985 Palm Springs Vintage Grand Prix.

Rodger Ward was one of those towering figures during what some now call the Golden Age of Racing, the fifties and sixties. Although Rodger is best known for his feats in Championship (Indianapolis-type) Cars, he drove in virtually every sort of auto: midgets, sprinters, stock cars, sports cars, Formula One and even hot rods (drag racing and speed runs on the dry lakes). Respect and admiration for his many feats made him one of racing's icons.

Unfailingly friendly and loquacious, for a number of years after his retirement from active racing, Rodger was known as the affable ambassador of racing.

Rodger Morris Ward was born in Beloit, Kansas, on January 10, 1921. The family moved to California in 1929, where Rodger's father opened a garage and wrecking yard in South Pasadena. As a youth, he helped his dad in the business and, at age 13, he built a Model T hot rod from junk parts long before the hot-rodding craze had taken hold.

Along came the war and Rodger joined the Army. Soon recognizing his ability, the military sent him to flight school, where he trained as a fighter pilot. The young lieutenant was anxious to see combat, but he turned out to be such an accomplished pilot that he was forced to spend the entire duration training others. He was an instructor on both P-38s and B-17s. Carroll Shelby, also in the Air Corps at the time, remembered Rodger training pilots at Wichita Falls, Texas. Later, Rodger was posted to Wright Field (now Wright-Patterson AFB) where another young lieutenant and future champion, Sam Hanks, was also serving.

Rodger started racing Midgets right after the war ended but while still in the service. He was stationed at Wichita Falls, Texas, when a quarter-mile dirt track was built. His commanding officer gave him the option of racing or flying. He chose racing and was discharged in 1946.

He continued to race as a civilian, and his first win was in a Midget in 1947 at Balboa Stadium in San Diego. In those days, top-line Midgets were powered by Offenhauser engines. Rodger's friend Vic Edelbrock installed a modified Ford V8–60 engine in his Midget. Ward shocked the Midget-racing world when he won with it at Gilmore Stadium in Los Angeles on August 10 and then won again the following night.

Rodger was instrumental in providing three major jaw-dropping shocks to the auto racing world. The first was the Gilmore Stadium 1950 race when he beat the Offies with a Ford V8–60. Next was at Lime Rock on July 25, 1959, where he beat the cream of the road racing fraternity in a circle track Offenhauser midget. Finally, he was instrumental in getting Jack Brabham's small mid-engined Cooper to Indianapolis and within a few years all Indy-Cars were mid-engined.

The story of the V8–60 at Gilmore was an example of the Greatest Generation's can-do, make-do, will-do attitude. The expensive Offenhauser engine, which had evolved from the Miller, was the sine qua non of top-tier American racing. In midgets they competed on the United Racing Association Blue Circuit. The lowly stock block Ford V8–60 was relegated to the second-class Red Circuit.

Rodger Ward with his BT-15 Vultee Valiant at Luke Field while in the army. Rodger Ward collection.

When Rodger showed up at Gilmore with Vic Edelbrock's hopped-up little Ford, the competition sniffed at it. When Rodger smoked them all, they took another whiff. To compete against the Offenhausers, Edelbrock had developed the use of nitro methane. It was legal but had a strange odor and required experimenting with fuel mixtures so as not to destroy the engine. The win rocketed Vic Edelbrock to prominence in the racing world.

Even with the nitro boost, Rodger had to work hard to beat the Offies. He was famous for running the high line against the "cushion" (a dirt berm thrown up by cars running the shorter lower line). Watching Rodger at a high-banked track like Culver

14. Rodger Ward

In 1948 Rodger won at the Orange Show Stadium in San Bernardino. Rodger Ward collection.

City dirt tracking his midget at full bore around the top edge of the track made you forget the price of admission.

In 1951 he won the AAA National Stock Car Championship and also competed at Indianapolis for the first time. In 1953, he won the U.S. National Champion (for Championship Cars, then called the Championship Trail). He was able to transition from traditional to roadster to mid-engined Championship Cars. He raced in the Indy 500 fifteen times and won twice (1959, 1962) and won the USAC National Championship twice (1959, 1962). He would have won Indy a third time but for a fluke. In all, Rodger's IndyCar record was 26 wins in 150 starts. He finished in the top ten in more than half of them. His last win was at Trenton in 1966. After Indy that year, he retired as a professional driver.

The Indianapolis 500 was part of the FIA World Championship from 1950 through 1960. Drivers competing at Indy during those years were credited with World Championship points. Rodger drove in 12 World Championship races, including ten starts at Indy plus the 1959 and the 1963 U.S. Grand Prix. All were in Offenhausers except the 1963, when he drove a Lotus 24 for Reg Parnell Racing.

During the Golden Age, Rodger was one of the few American professionals who ventured into sports car racing. I talked to him about it one time. He said,

> In the late fifties, I found I enjoyed road racing so much that I decided to buy my own car. I ended up getting a Cooper Monaco for about $10,000. I raced it at Riverside and then took it to the Bahamas Speed Week, where I scattered the Climax engine. So I replaced it with a small-block Buick V8."

A chance meeting developed into a friendship that changed the American racing world. When Rodger Ward met Jack Brabham at Sebring in 1959 he discovered that

Top: **The celebration for Rodger's second Indy 500 win in 1962. Rodger Ward collection.** *Bottom:* **Rodger Ward at the Indy 500 in 1962. Rodger Ward collection.**

both of their careers had begun with racing midgets on dirt. Jack had been a mechanic in the Australian Air Force and after the war had built an Australian-style midget for an American neighbor. The neighbor's wife refused to let him drive it, so Jack took over and won a championship. He continued to dominate the Aussie tracks for the next eight years. In 1955 he moved to England and took a job at the John Cooper Works. Cooper was building a motorcycle-engined Formula Three car and Jack took on the task of upsizing Cooper's output to larger sports cars and eventually Formula One cars.

It was one of these mid-engined Coopers that caught Rodger's attention at Sebring, and he suggested that Jack test it at Indianapolis. In 1960 Brabham was heading to Watkins Glen for the U.S. Grand Prix. He called Rodger to arrange a test of the Formula One car at Indy. Rodger enthusiastically made the arrangements and while at the Speedway drove several laps in the mid-engined Formula One car. When he climbed out, he exclaimed, "This is the future."

Rodger's first Indy 500 in a mid-engined car was the 1964 race where he drove A. J. Watson's creation powered by a Ford V8. He was the class of the field and felt he should have won by a mile. But, as has befallen all racers, last-minute decisions queered the deal. A change in fuel from gasoline to alcohol and a last-minute repositioning of the fuel selector valve resulted in Rodger making five pit stops to A. J. Foyt's three. Even after losing several minutes in the pits, he was only 84 seconds behind Foyt at the finish.

Jack Brabham credited Rodger and Masten Gregory with saving his life. In the 1964 Indy race, he and Rodger were both in new rear-engine cars. Jack said that Rodger had warned him about Mickey Thompson's car being unpredictably erratic and advised him not to get too close to it in traffic. Jack said he deliberately hung back far enough so that when the MacDonald-Saks fireball erupted, he was able to avoid it.

Even though Ward was famous for having won Indy, the race many remember him for was winning a Formula Libre event in 1959 at Lime Rock Park in a nine-year-old midget. Rodger remembered,

> The way I got the ride in the midget was when Chris Economaki and I were driving there from Syracuse. I had been invited to run the Lime Rock event but couldn't find anyone to let me drive their car. Chris said, "You know, Rodger, I know someone here on the East Coast who has one of the very best midgets. I think you might do well with it at Lime Rock, which is a rather tight course." I replied, "Economaki, I don't want to go there and embarrass myself." After meeting the car owner, however, I decided to give it a shot. After practice I was pleasantly surprised. Of course, it had only one gear. They ran the event in three heats. In the first heat, I was quicker than anyone else except down the long straight where George Constantine in his new Aston Martin smoked me off even though I could pass him anywhere else. After the first heat, I told the mechanics to bump the gear ratio, so I could go faster on the straight; from then on it wasn't even a contest. That was about as much fun as I ever had in a race. After I won, it was even more fun to see the look on John Fitch's face.

John Fitch wrote about that race:

> He blew off Fangio's World Championship 250 Maserati driven very well by Chuck Daigh plus George Constantine in an Aston Martin, Ricardo Rodriguez in a 3-liter Maserati and me

Rodger's last IndyCar race was in 1966 at Trenton. Rodger Ward collection.

in a Cooper Monaco. Others were many of the fast cars of the day, all with very good drivers. The consensus among old-time race fans was that this was Rodger's greatest race ever.

With that success under his belt, he entered the same midget in the Formula One at Sebring. But the long Sebring straights were not as well suited to the midget as was Lime Rock. That ended Rodger's road racing of the midget. In 1963, Rodger drove a Lotus-BRM for Reg Parnell at the U.S. Grand Prix at Watkins Glen, but he failed to finish because of a mechanical problem.

After retiring as a driver, Rodger designed, owned and operated the Owosso Speedway in Michigan. Also, he designed Indianapolis Raceway Park, a road course. When the now-defunct Ontario Motor Speedway opened, he served as its director of public relations. While there, always innovative, he conceived of and promoted Eight-Wheel Truck Racing. Later, he managed the Circus Circus unlimited hydroplane team.

Rodger was a commentator for ABC's *Wide World of Sports* for NASCAR and IndyCars from 1965 to 1970. From 1980 to 1985, he served as a driver expert for the Indianapolis Motor Speedway Radio Network.

During the Vietnam War, he toured combat areas, visiting with servicemen and showing films of Indianapolis races. Because of that activity, he became known as racing's ambassador of good will.

In 1985, we organized a vintage revival of the fifties- and sixties-era Palm Springs Road Races. I asked Rodger to drive my 1968 Gilbert IndyCar in the main event. To put on the 1985 Palm Springs, we formed a new club named Vintage Racing. Bobby Unser served a term as president, and then Rodger succeeded him. In addition to Palm Springs, we also raced at Riverside, Willow Springs, Texas and at Tacoma two times. A unique event was our open-road vintage races in Baja California. The course crossed the peninsula from Ensenada to San Felipe. Rodger worked very hard and took the job of president very seriously. We worked with a Mexican partner but eventually things there got out of control. During the third year, two participants were killed as well as a spectator. After the race, some of the Americans who had come to see the event

Rodger driving Art Evans' car at the 1985 Palm Springs vintage race. Rodger Ward collection.

would drive over the course like crazy persons. For us, safety became an issue over which we had little control, so we quit and Vintage Racing, which at one time had more than 1,000 members, eventually went out of business.

With the Mexico experience under his belt, Rodger somehow persuaded the authorities in Nevada to let him stage open-road racing. These events were not limited to vintage vehicles; virtually anyone could enter. The course went from Elko and ended near Las Vegas. He even put on open-road races in Texas.

For a time, Rodger and I had a little sideline business of buying, restoring and selling Miller and Offenhauser engines. Rodger's brother, Ron, had a small shop in Ontario, California, where we had the work done. For a while, we did quite well, but eventually the supply of old engines in need of repair ran out. At the time, I had a 1954 Lincoln Capri, the same make and model Rodger had driven in the 1954 Carrera Panamericana. He enjoyed tooling around town in it. Perhaps because of his Mexico experience, his favorite car was always a Lincoln.

During the nineties, Rodger and his wife, Sherrie, moved to San Diego when Rodger became the vice president of Composite Automobile Research. The company designed a very basic car for the third world and sold franchises for their construction.

The idea, while certainly viable on its face, would have, I think, required a much larger organization to make it profitable. For a time, the company's penny stocks soared, but they eventually tanked and Rodger left.

Afterwards, Rodger went to work for a large San Diego car dealer, Rug Cunningham (no relation to Briggs Cunningham). Rug was also a dedicated enthusiast who participated in vintage racing and helped, along with Rodger, to form the San Diego Automotive Museum. In addition to being an executive in Cunningham's business, he drove some of Rug's cars in vintage events.

The last time Rodger drove in a race was on June 13, 1999, at a celebrity race we put together using new Dodge Neons at a vintage event at the old blimp base in Tustin, California. In addition to Rodger, eight other champions joined the fray: Sir Jack Brabham, Tom Sneva, Roger Mears, Gene Felton, John Morton, Jerry Grant, Gordon Johncock and Kevin Cogan. Running nose to tail, they had the crowd on its feet with few of the Neons surviving without dents. Rodger's friend Sir Jack won.

Rodger in 1988. Photograph by Art Evans.

With failing health, Rodger had to retire at age 83; he died on July 5, 2004. We paid our last respects to Rodger on July 11 at the San Diego Automotive Museum in famed Balboa Park. Quite a few of us who were his friends traveled together by train from Los Angeles to San Diego. An overflow standing-room-only crowd of more than 300 showed up to pay tribute to his life and to his racing accomplishments. Packed from one end to the other, the building was filled with family, friends and fans. I was honored that Sherrie asked me to be one of the speakers.

15

Sam Hanks

During the early fifties, one of the biggest sports stars in the United States was Sam Hanks. Notice I said "sports," not "motorsports." He was one of the best-loved sports figures to come out of Southern California. For many of us enthralled with racing, he was our hero. He was one of those special people who come along only very rarely.

His racing career extended from 1932 through 1957, culminating in winning the Indianapolis 500. He was an advisor and referee for all of the Los Angeles Times Grand Prix and operated Southern California's first racing school with Ken Miles.

Samuel Dwight Hanks was born on July 13, 1914, in Columbus, Ohio. His father, a building contractor, moved the family to California in 1920 because there was more opportunity. Sam graduated from Alhambra High School and went on to a career in automobile racing and aircraft engineering. He had a distinguished career in the Army during World War II.

In 1930 Sam's father was driving a Ford Model T, when he was hit in the rear by a truck and received severe head injuries. He never fully recovered. Sam, at 16 years old and still in high school, became the family breadwinner.

At Alhambra High School, Sam was so good in shop and auto mechanics that he was appointed as a student instructor. While still in high school, Hanks got a job working on aircraft engines. He traded work for flying instruction. His interest in flying lasted his lifetime. He was one of the few championship-level racing drivers who also excelled as a mechanic and engineer.

After graduating from Alhambra High, Sam bought a Model A Ford and prepared it for racing. He raced it against the clock at Muroc Dry Lake (now the site of Edwards Air Force Base.) He began racing Midgets in 1936 at the two-year-old Gilmore Stadium in the West Hollywood area of Los Angeles. His first ride was a Midget powered by a 4-60 Evinrude outboard engine. Switching to an Offy-powered Midget, Sam won a lot of races as well as the 1937 Pacific Coast Midget Championship in the Offy. In those days, his 40 percent share of the winnings wasn't enough to support his family. The solution was to own his own car. So Sam worked as an engineer and purchased an Offy engine plus a Midget chassis. He got the engine from Fred Offenhauser on a handshake.

Sam was a man whose integrity was never questioned, and he paid Fred from his winnings. Entering races as a car owner, driver and mechanic, he won over 80 races through 1941 and garnered the National Midget Championship that year. He was one of the most successful Midget drivers of all time.

Sam Hanks in his Midget built by Roy Richter and powered by the 25th Offy engine built by Fred Offenhauser, Chicago, 1939. From 1937 through 1941, Sam won 80 feature races while doing all the mechanical work himself! Alice Hanks collection.

During the summer, California boys would trailer their Midgets through the Midwest racing at state fairs, on horse tracks and the new board track in Chicago, plus the oiled-clay quarter mile in Detroit. It was a seasonal bonanza. Sam won the first two races at Soldier Field and the Chicago Sportsman's Trophy in 1939. In 1940 he collected the VFW Motor City Speedway Championship in Detroit.

In 1940, Hanks drove in his first Indianapolis 500, finishing 13th. The last 50 laps were under the yellow flag in the rain. He won a grand total of $650. The next year, 1941, he entered Indy again, but was injured in an accident caused by a mechanical failure on Carburetion Day. Carburetion Day was used to re-tune fuel mixtures and make a spark plug selection to enable engines to produce maximum power for four laps. The engines had been leaned out to produce extra power for only the four laps of qualifying. Sam's tuning skill would serve the nation during World War II. This Carburetion Day accident was the only time he was ever injured in a racing accident, but what an accident it was! A connecting rod broke and locked up the rear wheels as the car approached the southwest turn. No seat belt, no roll bar, no fire protection on the car! Completely out of control at more than 120 mph, the car tore down 25 feet of guard rail and rolled several times, throwing Sam out. He sustained head and back injuries but was still able to answer the doctor's questions. Whenever a race driver is involved in an accident, the doctor queries him to determine the extent of brain injury. Questions like Who's the president? How do you spell your middle name? He spent a couple of days in the hospital.

Sam had stored his Midget, his source of a steady income, in a garage at the Speedway. While he was in the hospital there was a major fire on Gasoline Alley. Luckily some friends saved his Midget. Ignoring sore shoulders, he campaigned the Midget on the West Coast that summer in order to support his family.

When World War II started, Sam went to work at Lockheed Aircraft in Burbank, California, doing pre-flight check-outs on P-38s. In addition, he was on a team that installed water injection on Allison engines for P-38s and P-51s. Instead of extra power for qualifying a race car, the military wanted extra war emergency power to escape enemy bullets. An engine rated for 1,000 hours for time between overhauls might last 30 minutes when the throttle was pushed through the stops to war emergency power. The extra power was accomplished with water injection, alcohol, and turbo boost. The demand for military aircraft was critical, so they worked seven days a week and long hours.

Because of Sam's expertise on engines, in 1943 he received a direct commission as a second lieutenant in the Army Air Corps. First, he was assigned to officer training at a base in Florida. His next assignment was at Wright Field (now Wright-Patterson Air Force Base) in Dayton, Ohio, working on the development of Pratt and Whitney radial engines. Sam spent a lot of time in Hartford, Connecticut at the Pratt & Whitney

Sam was a warrant officer in the U.S. Army. This photograph was taken at Wright Field, Dayton, Ohio, in 1944. Alice Hanks collection.

plant. During World War II Wright-Patterson was the Air Force's primary R&D facility. They developed, manipulated and tested any idea that might improve the performance of military aircraft. One project was to commission Colonel Hal Dixon to fly a Spitfire across the North Atlantic from England so they could try to improve its range. Dixon was chosen for the mission because, pre-war, while he was in the RAF, he had flown Lockheed Hudson bombers to England pioneering the North Atlantic route. (Hal Dixon is the father of John Dixon, a contributor to this book.)

Sam's assignment at Wright, appropriate to his expertise, was to increase engine horsepower. One solution was to use water injection at full power with a lean mixture to prevent burning the pistons.

Dayton, Ohio, was not only the home of Air Force research but also the headquarters of National Cash Register. NCR developed and built the code-breaking machines for the Allies.

Interestingly enough and unbeknownst to one another, Carroll Shelby and John Fitch, both flying officers, were also at Wright Field at the same time as Sam during the war. While at Wright, Sam met an 18-year-old civil-service secretary working in the finance department, Alice Hedrick, and made a habit of stopping by her desk to share a cup of coffee. They became sweethearts, a relationship that lasted for a lifetime. Hanks mustered out as a first lieutenant in 1945. In July 1947, he and Alice were married.

After the war, Hanks resumed Midget racing. He won his first race after the four-year layoff on November 8, 1945, at the Los Angeles Coliseum. The car had been entered and was printed in the program with Danny Oakes driving. Sam was out of the Army and showed up in time to take over the car and win the race. Sam's recent experience testing high-performance fuels in the Air Corps enabled him to formulate a fuel for his midget's engine so that he could get maximum power for 250 laps. The coliseum had been built for the 1932 Olympics and could seat 100,000 people. After little Gilmore Stadium's capacity of 18,000, what a magnificent display it was when, in 1947, a record 65,000 spectators watched Sam Hanks win a 250-mile race. Sam won the Pacific Coast Midget Championship in 1946 and the National AAA Championship in 1949. The American Automobile Association sanctioned major automobile racing in the United States from 1905 to 1955. Hanks drove his very last Midget race in 1952. He was the biggest ever money winner as owner, driver and mechanic.

In 1954, Sam partnered with Ray Nichels to set a world's closed course speed record of 182.554 mph driving a Firestone Tire and Rubber Company test car at the Chrysler Proving Grounds in Chelsea, Michigan. The car was a Nichels-prepared Chrysler Hemi V8-powered Kurtis-Kraft roadster.

Racing resumed at Indy after the war in 1946. That year, Sam qualified Gordon Schroeder's Spike Jones Special on the front row. Spike Jones was the celebrity band

Opposite, top: **In 1946, Hanks won the Pacific Coast Midget Championship at the Los Angeles Coliseum.** *Bottom:* **Sam won a 250-lap race at Los Angeles Coliseum on November 8, 1945. Both photographs, Alice Hanks collection.**

15. Sam Hanks

leader–comedian that sponsored Midgets and Indy cars. The car had a unique engine, a Sampson V16. It was basically two Miller 91s ingeniously cobbled together to produce a 180-cubic-inch super-charged engine. Unfortunately, it blew an oil line after only 18 laps. (Alden L. Sampson II was a wealthy Massachusetts manufacturer that owned Louis Meyer's first winning Indy car in 1928). Sam was dejectedly watching the race when Joie Chitwood pulled in with physical problems. An eager Hanks hopped into Joie's car and drove it to a remarkable, but uncredited for Sam, fifth place. He did receive 128 points for his effort.

For the next 12 years, Hanks competed in Champ Cars. In 1952 he placed third at Indy and was also third in the National Championship. In 1953 he was again third at Indy and won the AAA National Champion.

At Indy, he placed second in 1956. Also in 1956 he competed in two stock car road races at Pomona and Paramount Ranch, winning both.

Sam in a Bill Stroppe-prepared Mercury (9) at the 1956 stock car race at Paramount Ranch. Photograph by Art Evans.

leader–comedian that sponsored Midgets and Indy cars. The car had a unique engine, a Sampson V16. It was basically two Miller 91s ingenuously cobbled together to produce a 180-cubic-inch super-charged engine. Unfortunately, it blew an oil line after only 18 laps. (Alden L. Sampson II was a wealthy Massachusetts manufacturer that owned Louis Meyer's first winning Indy car in 1928). Sam was dejectedly watching the race when Joie Chitwood pulled in with physical problems. An eager Hanks hopped into Joie's car and drove it to a remarkable, but uncredited for Sam, fifth place. He did receive 128 points for his effort.

For the next 12 years, Hanks competed in Champ Cars. In 1952 he placed third at Indy and was also third in the National Championship. In 1953 he was again third at Indy and won the AAA National Champion.

At Indy, he placed second in 1956. Also in 1956 he competed in two stock car road races at Pomona and Paramount Ranch, winning both.

Sam in a Bill Stroppe-prepared Mercury (9) at the 1956 stock car race at Paramount Ranch. Photograph by Art Evans.

15. Sam Hanks

Sam Hanks, an old man by the race track standards of the day, had decided to retire after the 1956 Indy 500. George Salih, an old friend, cornered him and convinced Sam that he and Howard Gilbert had built a car in the garage at his home in Whittier, California that *would* win Indy. With a great leap of faith and respect for a trusted friend, Sam postponed retirement, drove the car and achieved the dream of his lifetime—winning the Indianapolis 500!

The car, the Belond Exhaust Special, was the first laydown roadster where the Offy engine was laid on its side to reduce frontal area and hence drag.

After the race, Sam said, "I'd been dreaming about winning Indy for 17 years—ever since I first went there in 1940—so when I finally won it, I decided it was time to hang up my goggles for keeps." He was 43 years old in an era when racing was so dangerous that many drivers didn't live to 40. While drinking milk in Victory Lane, he told the cheering throng, "Ladies and gentlemen, I've loved every minute I've been here, but this is my last one."

It didn't turn out to be the last time Sam drove in competition. He had a contractual obligation to Ford, which he honored. He drove stock cars for the rest of that year and won the Pacific Coast Championship. As a matter of fact, Hanks was probably as good on road courses as he was on ovals, but he was prevented from entering sports car races due to his professional status. In those days, the Sports Car Club of America was simon-pure and didn't allow pros to compete with its amateur members. Even so, Sam was often seen at Southern California events. At Palm Springs in 1953, he drove an obsolete Formula One car in an exhibition and did 161.48 mph on the back straight, setting a track record. The best speed that winner Jack McAfee in a Ferrari could do was 142.85 mph. Sam was a close friend of Culver City Buick dealer Bill Murphy, so he often wrenched and advised Bill at the wheel of his Kurtis sports car.

After Sam's retirement, Tony Hulman appointed Sam as director of racing at Indianapolis, a position he held until 1979. He drove the pace car at the Indianapolis 500 from 1958 to 1963. Back in California he was also director of racing for *Los Angeles Times*–sponsored races at Riverside and Ontario from 1958 through 1980. Sam drove the pace car at the *Los Angeles Times* races at Riverside for 25 years. He also served as a consultant for Raybestos Brakes and

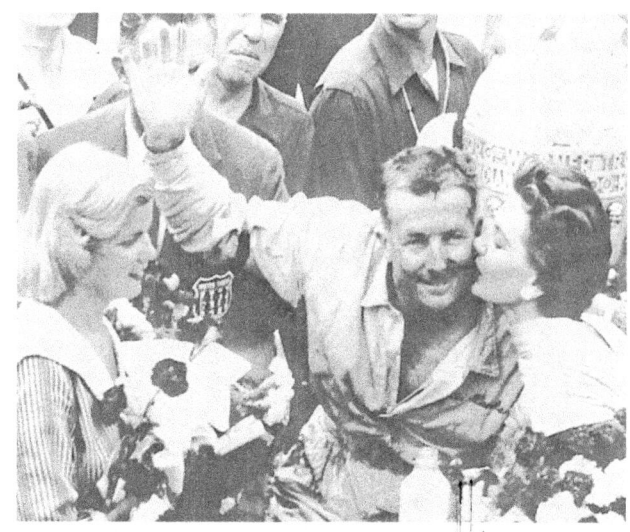

Sam celebrates winning the 1957 Indy 500. Race queen and actress Cyd Charisse kisses him while his wife, Alice, looks on. Alice Hanks collection.

Monroe Shock Absorbers. He and Ken Miles operated one of the first-ever racing drivers' schools at Mile Square, a wartime airfield, in Orange County.

Sam Hanks was elected into a grand total of six halls of fame. He continued his interest in aviation by flying Mach 1.2 in a Northrop T-38 with Chuck Yeager. He upped that to Mach 2.1—1,500 mph—in an F-104 at Edwards Air Force Base in 1968. Sam was an active member of the Quiet Birdmen, the Professional Race Pilots Association and was on the Contest Committee for the National Championship Air Races.

Nostalgia is the emotional warm puppy for old warriors. Sam said that despite all the celebrity, awards, and accolades he had earned, the years he raced his own Midget as owner, driver, and mechanic with his beloved wife, Alice, by his side, held a special place in his heart.

In retirement, Sam and Alice lived in Pacific Palisades in a home overlooking the Santa Monica Bay and the Pacific Ocean. There was a constant flow of visitors and invitations that continues, for Alice, to this day. In his later years, Sam and I became closer friends. Alice was still working as an executive secretary and Sam could no longer drive, so I would frequently visit him at their home, plus we also talked frequently on the phone. I took Sam's portrait in the front yard of their home in 1988.

Sam died on June 27, 1994. A memorial service was held in a hotel ballroom adjacent to the

Top: **Sam Hanks at home in Pacific Palisades, California, in 1988.** *Bottom:* **Alice and Sam at home in Pacific Palisades in 1990. Photographs by the author.**

runway at the Van Nuys Airport on July 9, 1994. It was attended by hundreds of friends and fans who loved Sam. Many Quiet Birdmen and race aficionados were present. A missing-man formation composed of World War II fighter aircraft flew over the airport. They were so low that their rivets were visible from the ground. The hotel shook and, finally, tears came. I was proud that Alice had a 16" × 20" print of my portrait of Sam displayed in the front of the room at the memorial service.

There are those of us who will never forget Sam. He remains in our hearts.

16

Steve McQueen

Steve McQueen was a movie star whose celebrity has lived way beyond his lifetime. A documentary film was released in 2015 titled *Steve McQueen, the Man and Le Mans*. In 2017, a movie of his life story, *Steve McQueen: American Icon*, was shown in select theaters. And during that same year, a new book was published, *Steve McQueen: Le Mans in the Rearview Mirror* by Don Nunley with Marshall Terrill.

While writing this, I wondered why Steve's legacy seems to be so long-lived. I asked my son, who was one year old when McQueen died, if he had ever heard of Steve McQueen. He replied, "Yes, what I remember is that [1968] movie [*Bullitt*] where he drove a Mustang like crazy all over San Francisco." I asked when he had seen the film. He said he didn't think he ever had. Asking others of that generation, it appears that all sorts of young people have heard of McQueen. He was so popular that he was always in demand by directors and producers. Consequently, he could ask for and receive large compensation.

This American actor was called the King of Cool. He was a top box-office draw during the 1960s and 1970s. His best-known film was probably *Bullitt*, for which he was nominated for an Academy Award as best actor. He was also nominated as best actor for a Golden Globe Award and was selected as best actor for his role in the 1963 film *The Great Escape* at the Moscow International Film Festival.

Terence Steven McQueen was born on March 24, 1930, in Beech Grove, Indiana, a suburb of Indianapolis. Steve had a very troubled childhood. Six months after their marriage, Steve's father left his pregnant wife to join a flying circus and was never heard from again. His mother, an alcoholic, wasn't able to care for her young child and left him with her parents in 1933. Steve and his grandparents moved in with his grandmother's brother on his farm in Slater, Missouri. The brother, Steve remembered, "was a very good man, very strong, very fair." He gave Steve a red tricycle for his fourth birthday.

When he was eight, his mother took Steve to live with her and a new husband in Indianapolis. Steve recalled that, when he left the farm, "Uncle Claude gave me a personal going-away present, a gold watch, with an inscription inside that read, 'To Steve, who has been like a son to me.'"

Steve had had an ear infection that left him partially deaf, and he didn't get along well in the new environment. His new stepfather often beat him. When he was nine, he ran away and lived on the streets, joined a gang and indulged in petty crime. His mother sent him back to the farm in Slater. His mother had divorced number two and moved to Los Angeles, where she married a third husband. She again had Steve returned to her. In a repeat of the previous stepfather, the new one beat not only Steve but also his wife. So Steve left and returned again to the Slater farm.

At 14, he suddenly left the farm and joined a circus. Then he went back to his mother in Los Angeles and rejoined a gang. When the police caught him stealing hubcaps, he was returned to his mother. After the stepfather beat him and threw him down the stairs, Steve said, "You lay your stinkin' hands on me again and I swear, I'll kill ya."

Claiming he was incorrigible, his mother obtained a court order that sent him to the California Junior Boys Republic in Chino. While there he became more mature and was elected to the Boys' Council, which set rules for the boys. He left when he turned 16 and returned to live with his mother, who was then living in Greenwich Village, New York. Much later in life when Steve had become famous, he returned now and then to the school to talk with the boys. It was a lifelong association.

While in New York, he had met two sailors who were in the merchant marine. So he volunteered during World War II to serve on a ship going to the Dominican Republic. Arriving there, he jumped ship and got a job in a brothel. Then he drifted to Texas and went from job to job, including as a roughneck, a carnival barker and a lumberjack.

When he was 17, he remarked, "it was all very pleasant just lying in the sun and watching the girls go by, but one day I suddenly felt bored with hanging around and went and joined the Marines."

After basic training, he was assigned to a tank unit and promoted to private first class. But because of his undisciplined behavior, he was demoted to private. On a weekend pass, he failed to return to the post, spending two weeks with his girlfriend. After being arrested by the Shore Patrol, he spent over a month in the brig. While there, he determined that he would change his lifestyle, to adopt Marine Corps values and improve himself.

When he was released, he rejoined his unit on a ship that was training in the Arctic. Suddenly, the ship hit a sandbank. Several tanks and their crews were thrown into the freezing water. A number of the men drowned, but Steve jumped in and saved five of them.

Because of his heroism, Steve was assigned to the Honor Guard that protected President Truman's yacht. After his discharge in 1950, Steve said, "The Marines gave me discipline I could live with. By the time I got out, I could deal with things on a more realistic level. All in all, despite my problems, I liked my time in the Marines."

In addition to serving in the Marine Corps he was a top motorcycle and sports-car race driver. After leaving the corps, Steve, with financial help from the G.I. Bill, studied acting at Sanford Meisner's Neighborhood Playhouse in New York. His first role was in a 1952 play. He had one line, spoken in Yiddish, "Alts izfarloyrn" (All is lost). He also studied acting in a class taught by Stella Adler.

In order to get some money, he raced motorcycles at the Long Island City Raceway. He was good at it and able to win about $100 almost every weekend.

During the early 1950s, Steve appeared in some minor parts in plays in New York. He debuted on Broadway in the 1955 play *A Hatful of Rain*, starring Ben Gazzara. Later that year, he relocated to Hollywood to give it a try. His first role was on television in *Westinghouse Studio One*. His first film appearance was a small part in *Somebody Up There Likes Me*, starring Paul Newman. From there, he starred in a number of television series. The most successful was *Wanted: Dead or Alive*.

In 1956, Steve married actress Neile Adams. They had a daughter, Terry Leslie, in 1959 and a son, Chad, born in 1960. Steve and Neile were divorced in 1972.

Steve continued racing motorcycles and started sports car road racing in his own Porsche 356 Super Speedster after some coaching from future Formula One driver Ronnie Bucknum. His first race was at Santa Barbara on May 30, 1959, where he placed 11th in a preliminary production-car event. In the main event for that group he was a winner!

Steve's next race was at Hourglass Field on June 21 near San Diego. I remember it well because I was the assistant race chairman. Sometime during practice, Steve came rushing up to me with some sort of a complaint. It was so long ago that now I don't even remember what it was about. Eventually we came to some sort of a resolution and Steve went off to race. His 356 Porsche threw a rod, so the car didn't run. Earl Callicut gave Steve a ride in the Porsche Carrera and he managed a third overall in the Consolation Race. He ran in two more events during 1959, scoring a second at another Santa Barbara race and sixth at Del Mar.

In 1963, Steve McQueen (right) came to visit Carroll Shelby at the Shelby American facility in Venice, California. They discussed Steve buying a Cobra and the two took a drive with McQueen at the wheel. In the end, Steve didn't buy one. Photograph by the author.

Steve became well known after his leading role in *Wanted: Dead or Alive*, a 94-episode television series that ran from 1958 and into 1961. It was a big break for Steve when Frank Sinatra chose him for a major role in *Never So Few*. During the sixties, Steve starred in hugely successful films, including *The Great Escape*, *Love with the Proper Stranger*, *The Sand Pebbles* and *Bullitt*. The *Sand Pebbles* role was a perfect fit for his real-life persona. The character, Jake Holman, has true feelings for machinery. He talks to the ship's engine as if it were a buddy.

In 1971, Steve starred in the famous racing drama *Le Mans*. He and Paul Newman were reunited in *The Towering Inferno*, which became a tremendous box-office success. It was during this time that I ran into Steve again. He had come to my best-friend Jim Peterson's home in Altadena to buy Jim's XKSS Jaguar. After a lot of chitchat, I took a picture of them and the car. There is a third guy in the photo, but I don't remember his name. He had come with Steve to drive Steve's car home. Last I heard, the car was still owned by the McQueen family.

During the seventies, Steve was second overall and first in class driving a Porsche 908 at the March 21, 1970, 12 Hours of Sebring, America's premier road race. Next came

(Left to right) Unidentified, Steve McQueen and Jim Peterson. McQueen visited Jim's home in Altadena to buy Jim's XKSS Jaguar. The XKSS was a roadgoing version of the racing D-Type Jaguar. Photograph by the author.

the big daddy of them all, the 24 Hours of Le Mans. McQueen is listed as one of the drivers in a Porsche 908 that finished ninth overall. This pretty much concluded Steve's time as an auto racer, although he continued to race motorcycles. In 1971, he starred in the famous documentary about motorcycles *On Any Sunday*.

Well-known actress Ali MacGraw and Steve were married in 1973. They met when they starred together in the movie *The Getaway*. Ali had a miscarriage during the marriage, which ended in 1978. In 1979, a year before his death in 1980, McQueen married a model, Barbara Minty. Under her influence, Steve became an Evangelical Christian and attended a local church.

McQueen, a heavy smoker, developed a persistent cough in 1978. Even though he had given up cigarettes and had treatments, the cough persisted and he had shortness of breath. In December 1979, his doctor told him he had pleural mesothelioma, an incurable form of cancer. Steve had heard that there was a treatment for the cancer in Mexico. So he went to Rosarito Beach, even though his U.S. doctors had told him there was no treatment. He stayed there for three months, but the cancer got worse. I remember at the time that the talk in the racing community was about his Mexico venture.

When he returned to California in October, it was revealed that he had developed a large tumor on his liver. Even though his doctors told him it was inoperable, he returned to Mexico to have surgery for its removal. On November 7, 1980, Terence Steven McQueen died of cardiac arrest right after the operation. He was only 50 years old.

With few exceptions—Frank Sinatra and Stirling Moss come to mind—most others of his generation in entertainment and racing are sometimes not that well remembered by succeeding generations. Steve McQueen's legacy lives on. He was, in fact, a unique personality and is recalled by many. The 2005 *TV Guide* list of the Sexiest Stars of All Time included his name. His film *Bullitt* and Ford Mustangs are forever linked. Ford used his likeness (a double) in a 2005 commercial. The sunglasses he wore in *The Thomas Crown Affair* were auctioned off for $70,200 in 2006. His Rolex Explorer II watch sold for $234,000 in 2009. And his 1963 Ferrari fetched $2.31 million. Until 2011, Steve's 1957 Chevrolet convertible and his XKSS Jaguar were on display at the Petersen Automotive Museum.

Steve McQueen at Torrey Pines in 1956. Photograph by the author.

17

Ginny Sims

When the subject of the Greatest Generation comes up, we usually think of the heroism of John Wayne types engaged in World War II combat. Two of the men in this book, Ed Hugus and Chuck Daigh, exemplified that role as paratroopers making dangerous jumps, Hugus on Corregidor in the Pacific and Daigh during Operation Anvil/Dragoon in Europe. There were two women who qualified for almost every category of great. Mary Davis served in the Marine Corps and Ginny Sims in the Navy.

Less acclaimed are the women who were then called Rosie the Riveter. They worked in our factories while the men were off fighting.

Ginny Sims's claim to membership in the Greatest Generation included working as a Rosie the Riveter while operating an engine lathe machining aircraft landing gears. Later she was a U.S. Navy machinist's mate installing aircraft engines. In civilian life, she was a mother, a Los Angeles police officer, and a motion picture film cutter. While busy fulfilling these roles, in 1956 she bought a sports car and went racing!

Ginny's mother lived through the San Francisco earthquake of 1906 and then moved south to Los Angeles where she married. On February 5, 1921, Virginia Marie Jeffers was born to Jack V. and Hipolita Jeffers.

Ginny was born and raised at ground zero of the hot rod and race car development world that existed in Southern California between the two world wars. As the child of a carburetor specialist, she was raised in a male-oriented world and developed into a tall feminine beauty with a dose of masculinity in her character.

The Los Angeles area then had over 20 race tracks and a dozen air fields. Beverly Hills had both a race track and an airfield on Wilshire Boulevard across from today's Rodeo Drive luxury boutiques and the Beverly Wilshire Hotel.

Ginny's father, Jack V. Jeffers, owned the Carburetor Equipment Company in central Los Angeles and was a contemporary of Harry Miller. Miller also manufactured carburetors before designing the most winning engine in American racing history. The Miller engine evolved into the Offenhauser and was a winner for over 50 years, from the 1920s through the 1970s.

Jack Jeffers, like all fabricators, knew how to improvise. Not having a son, he taught his oldest daughter how to operate every machine in his shop. Ginny did this guy thing while growing to be a 5'8" brunette beauty and attending Hollywood High School. She could be considered a true hybrid and was a feminist with a take-no-prisoners attitude when it came to her plans.

The life-changing moment for Ginny occurred when her classmate Hammy offered to give her and her girlfriends a ride in his big red Buick convertible. He took them up to his family's estate near the entrance to Griffith Park. Hammy turned out to be the son of the Hamburger family, which built the largest department store west of the Mississippi.

The Hamburger family estate had spacious grounds with an elevated swimming pool deck plus garages across the driveway on a lower level. While taking in the panoramic view of 1930s Los Angeles, Ginny dropped her gaze to the garages and spotted a 6'2" handsome hunk working on Hammy's hot rod. She immediately insisted that Hammy introduce him and thus met her future husband, Frank Sims.

That began her teenage hot rod adventure. The object was to take a 1920s–1930s Ford Model A or B and modify the engine or install a V8, take it to the Southern California Timing Association event at Muroc Dry Lake and clock over 100 mph.

The time trials were the ultimate weekend for California performance car enthusiasts. The drill was to camp out Friday on the lake bed by a fire with the still desert air broken by song and coyote howls. After a glorious desert sunrise, the racing would begin.

The course was three or four miles depending on surface conditions: a two-mile run to the traps and a one-mile shutdown. You couldn't see the starting line because of the dusty haze kicked up by the racers. The '32 Ford grille on most roadsters would whistle at about 100 mph. The whistle would change tone with speed so you'd know when a hot one was coming through. The pre-war record was 140 mph turned by a highly modified Chevy four-banger in a special-bodied lakester.

For anyone with a little money, Southern California was a paradise during the 1920s, even during the economically depressed 1930s.

Ginny and Frank attended midget races at Ascot, Gilmore and Saugus (Bonelli) Stadiums and prepared cars for the dry lakes speed trials. They were married in 1942.

When the buildup to war began, she

Ginny Sims, shown here in 1944, served in the U.S. Navy during World War II. Ginny Sims collection.

took a job at Menasco Manufacturing in Burbank, where she operated an engine lathe machining landing gear for P-38 Lightnings and P-51 Mustangs. Ginny had a proclivity to be where the action was and felt a duty to her country, so when the Navy began enlisting women, Ginny signed up.

Ginny endured boot camp in Washington, D.C., and the Bronx, New York City. When it came time for assignment, she asked for duty as a machinist's mate. The officer looked at the 5'8" beauty and with dropped jaw asked, "Why?" She said, "I aced the mechanical aptitude test." She received a doubting, "I'll check that out." She got the assignment. She was sent to machinist school in Tennessee and Oklahoma. After school, she was posted to Alameda Naval Air Station in the San Francisco Bay where her job was installing engines on naval combat aircraft.

Frank had enlisted in the Army as a private and was discharged in 1945 as a major after clandestine duty in Southern China where the Office of Strategic Services (OSS), predecessor to the CIA, operated out of Kunming and was involved with French-Vietnamese politics. Julia Child, the famous chef, had worked for the OSS at that station.

In the spring of 1944, Machinist's Mate Sims, having been separated from Frank for over a year, got five-day leave to visit him at his camp in Fresno, California. After their soiree in the raisin capital, Ginny returned to Alameda carrying a little grape of her own. The Navy could accept female mechanics but drew the line at pregnant ones, so she was discharged.

Back in civilian life, after the birth of her daughter, Frances Ann, on January 8, 1945, Ginny decided she still needed meaningful excitement. She joined the Los Angeles Police Force. Three years later and after many depressing assignments dealing with the city's unfortunate juveniles, she left the force. She got a job at Technicolor where she strung three film strips together to make color prints. Three years of that was enough and she moved down the street to Paramount Pictures on Melrose. At Paramount she cut the edited film to make projection reels. Negative cutting became a 30-year profession.

A sedentary life wasn't satisfying to an active lady, so when she fell in with some sports car enthusiasts at their local watering hole, the Coach & Horses, she wanted to buy a sports car.

Ginny said,

> In 1955, I was the not so proud owner of a brown Hudson. Damn, that car was ugly, but it was rapid and reliable. It was named the "Brown Badoodoo." I'd sit in it and watch all those cute little English cars whiz by and suddenly I had a huge urge. I wanted an MGTD.
>
> The search began, and I found a little beauty on Ventura Blvd. at a dealership. I had my dream. It was white, with red wheels and upholstery, and a red plaid top and tonneau cover. What a beauty!
>
> It was not very long until I started going on rallies, and that was a new kick. We would start at the Coach & Horses on Sunset Blvd. and end there. It was a nice group of people and everyone had a sports car. I rallied for a few months and listened to their chatter about weekend races. This caught my interest and I decided to visit one of these events.
>
> One Sunday I drove out to Willow Springs to see my first race. There were left and right

turns, and the course went uphill and downhill. I had only been to races at Gilmore Stadium and Saugus where the tracks were oval. This was all new and so exciting, and there was a ladies' race too. You can well imagine the mind trip I was having. I started asking questions: "Where and how do you get into this new sport?"

The Southern California Sports Car Club was the answer. I arrived there and had my first meeting with Mary Hefley (later O'Connor), the secretary for the club. I filled out paperwork, showed a valid driver's license and was given a doctor's address to have a physical. Everything turned out O.K. and I was on my way to my first race in February 1956. The place was Goleta, just north of Santa Barbara.

Someone loaned me an old helmet. It resembled a bowl with leather covering the back of my head and strapping under my chin. There were no seat belts and who had ever heard of a roll bar?

Thursday night before the race, all cars had to be inspected. My car passed, and the excitement was growing. My car number was 95. I had bought red plaid stickum paper and cut out my number for the doors. My mechanic, Ted Swendsen, was like a kid brother to me and my two sisters. He performed all the necessary mechanical changes the car needed for #95 to pass its first inspection.

Friday night we left for Santa Barbara and stayed overnight in a motel. Ted and his girlfriend and Dale Warner and myself. Up early next morning and off to Goleta to get our first view of the track. It turned out to be an airport course with hay bales marking the corners. The straightaways were obvious. We found our pit and settled in. Ted did the last-minute tuning and we were set to go.

Ginny Sims drove Art Evans' Devin SS in the Ladies' Race on June 9, 1959, at Santa Barbara. Photograph by the author.

17. Ginny Sims

We watched the men's races and enjoyed seeing different classes of cars speeding by. The ladies' race encompassed all classes in the one race, from a small MG to a Porsche Spyder, Jaguar and Aston Martin. In my first race there would be 25 ladies driving.

Finally, it was time for the ladies' race. My car was driven to the starting lineup and I was in last place as I was a rookie. Looking at those 24 cars in front of me, my heart was beating fast. I could hardly wait for the green flag to drop. Ted gave me a pat on the helmet and the grid was cleared.

The flag dropped, and I took off. I negotiated all the turns and passed five cars in our 12-lap race. It was obvious I had a lead foot. When I drove into the pits I was overjoyed with my 20th place finish.

I drove the MG in three or four more races, and then decided to buy a little larger car. Ted helped me with the buy. It was purchased at the store where he worked as a top mechanic in Studio City. I was now the proud owner of a 1956 Triumph TR3.

We raced once a month at a track in Southern California. I had picked up a couple of trophies for winning in my class and soon I was invited to drive other people's cars. The first was a Morgan at Paramount Ranch. Then came an invite from a dealership to drive a Corvette.

After I had gained some experience, I drove the Harry Mann Corvette in the ladies' race and Bob Bondurant drove it in the men's race. This was the best so far. Later I drove a Talbot Lago that had been driven by Juan Fangio, five-time World Champion. It was a privately-owned racer and not up to the standards of a dealership car, but even so, it was great fun. It had a pre-selector transmission. On the dashboard was the selector with 1st thru 5th gear points. If you wanted to shift down, you moved the lever to the option and popped the clutch. Much easier than the conventional gear box. But the car blew its engine and I had a DNF (Did Not Finish).

Another car I drove was Art Evans' Devin with a huge Chevy engine. This is the racer that earned me the "Fastest Woman of the Year" Award in 1959 at Riverside Raceway. I turned 163.34 mph down the back straight. Of course, this is my favorite trophy.

Nineteen fifty-seven saw the ad-agencies for the car companies watching the ladies' races. A new concept had been thought up. Ladies would be driving in the Mobil Economy Run. Since the early 30s only men had driven in this event in which my father had been a participant. I was the 1st second-generation person to be entered.

Mary Davis was the first female picked as a driver and she chose me to be her navigator. I was honored. We had become great friends during our racing years. Now came the detuning. How to drive for the best economy. And while Mary was learning this strategy, I was taught to nav-

Ginny Sims (left) and Mary Davis in the 1957 Mobilgas Economy Run. Ginny Sims collection.

Ginny Sims (left) and Mary Davis won the Mobilgas Economy Run in 1957. Ginny Sims collection.

igate. My job was to keep her on time and on the right road. We won our class in a Plymouth V8 in a four-day race from Los Angeles to Sun Valley, Idaho. Much ado followed: TV appearances, newspaper ads and stories. We visited all the Los Angeles Plymouth dealers to tell our story for a month. Also, mink stoles and diamond watches for a job well done.

Mobilgas had always used racing to promote their products. They gave free gasoline to the racers and handed out their flying red horse decals for the cars. In 1936, when fuel economy became an issue, they came up with the Mobilgas Economy Run. With the auto industry ramping up their marketing directed at women, in 1957 Mobil decided to include women drivers. Mary Davis and Ginny Sims became their concession to the feminists, and the two ended up beating the men on their first run. Mary and Ginny did the Run as driver and navigator for the first five years. After that, Mary dropped out to develop Portofino Marina in Redondo Beach, California. Ginny continued as a successful Run driver for another six years.

Ginny went on to say,

I raced sports cars until 1961 and did Economy runs until 1968. The last Run ended at Indy due to the death of Martin Luther King and the ensuing riots in Washington, DC, which would have been our next stop. New York City was to be the final destination, but that was not to be. We were entertained royally at the track, and we drove our Run cars around the 2½ mile course. The Indy drivers took us for rides in their racers, and believe me, that got your heart started.

That was the end of my auto experiences but the friendships I made during those years have lasted a lifetime. It's unbelievable to think that that little car could lead to such adventure and fame.

During the 1950s a unique feminine "Three Musketeers" was formed composed of Ginny Sims, Mary Davis and Mary O'Connor. These three tall, stately women of impressive talents formed an inseparable comradeship that endured a lifetime. Beginning in the 1950s, until death intervened, these three ladies of distinction could be seen holding court at their table during dinner-awards ceremonies held in Southern California.

Mary Davis, racer, restaurateur and marina developer, is featured elsewhere in this book. Mary O'Connor is somewhat unsung but played a critical role in the ultimate success of the California Sports Car Club, where the international racing careers of many Americans began. Bill Pollack, Dan Gurney, Bob Bondurant and Jay Chamberlain come to mind. Mary made the club's events happen and was track mother and confidante to the drivers. Working as the executive director, Mary ran the business end of the office for Ken Miles, Bill Pollack and other early leaders of the Cal Club. She was so good at what she did that Hugh Hefner hired her to manage the Playboy Mansion, first in Chicago, then in Los Angeles. It was a lifetime career. She was featured in Hefner's TV biography. At one point during the filming she shed some tears. The producer promised her he would cut the scene. As is usual for Hollywood, he broke the promise, and Mary can be seen shedding sentimental tears on camera. Mary O'Connor spent over 40 years at Hefner's side as his most trusted and beloved assistant. She passed away at age 84 on January 27, 2013.

Ginny Sims drove in many Ladies' Races during the 1950s. This photograph was taken at the Santa Barbara airport in 1967. Ginny Sims collection.

Ginny Sims. Photograph by the author.

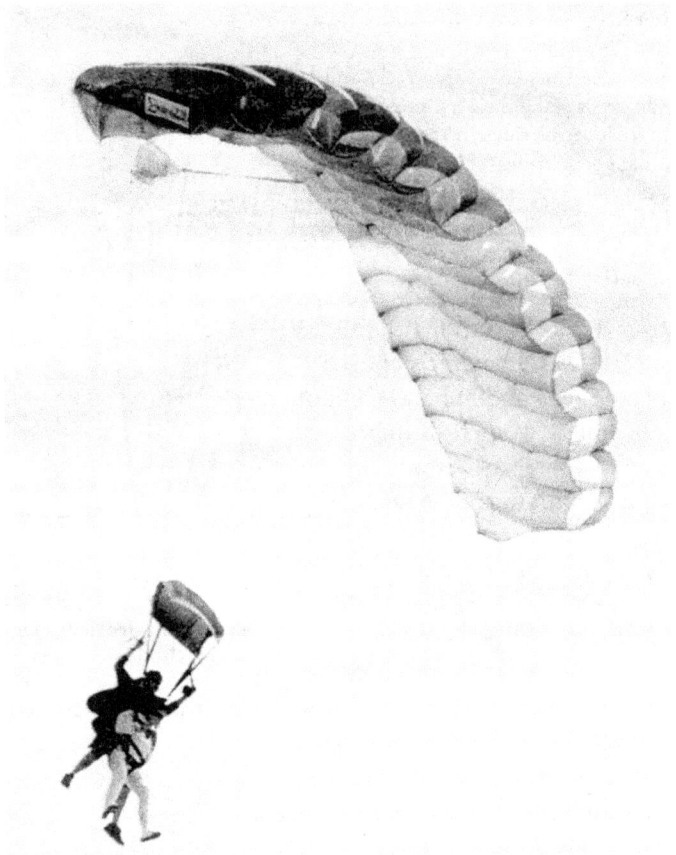

Ginny Sims celebrated her 90th birthday by jumping from an airplane over the Valley area of Los Angeles in 2011. Ginny Sims collection.

When Major Frank Sims returned from World War II, he had become too orderly for an emancipated woman who was unaccustomed to meeting masculine needs on demand. Frank had become an oil company executive and spent much time away from home. They parted company, and Ginny raised her daughter, Frances Ann, and pursued life as a modern woman. In retirement she occupied herself with grandmotherly things along with travel, gardening and attending Navy and racing reunions. She now lives in a retirement home in Tarzana, California, and is lovingly attended by her grandson, Sacha Riviere, and his wife, Nicole, and four great-grandchildren. On her 90th birthday, to complete her bucket list she added skydiving to her resume by jumping out of an airplane.

At 97, Ginny is still vivacious, witty, and a strong and interesting personality. Without angst or anger, Ginny and her pals should be the role model for today's angry young women. They were liberal, and they lived the life they wanted without playing the victim card. They were truly women of the Greatest Generation.

18

Shav Glick

Most of those profiled in this book were, among other things, race drivers. The one exception is Shav Glick. Shav was a widely renowned sports journalist. While he covered other sports, his forte and love was motorsports. In 1994, he was inducted into the Motorsports Hall of Fame, the first newspaper writer to earn that honor. Mario Andretti remarked, "He was *the* authority. You wanted to be noticed by Shav Glick. He certainly had my respect." He wrote his first published story when he was only 14 years old. It was for the *Pasadena Post*. When he retired in 2006, he was 85.

Shavenau (no middle name) Glick was born on September 16, 1920, in Pasadena, California. He attended Pasadena Junior College. In those days, the two-year college included the last two years of high school. While a student, he was the editor of the school newspaper, the *PJC Chronicle*. He was also on the baseball team along with his classmate, Jackie Robinson. He played against Ted Williams. They were friends he later wrote about.

Shav wrote about one of his childhood memories: "In 1926, when I was five years old, at the 36th Annual Rose Parade in Pasadena, a wooden grandstand seating hundreds of people collapsed. Both of my parents suffered broken feet and ankles, but I was tossed up, sort of like a cork from a bottle and was one of the few people uninjured."

After graduation, Shav went to the University of California at Berkeley for his last two years of college. He continued in journalism and was the assistant editor of the *Daily Californian*. Shav graduated in 1942 with a degree in history. His first job while World War II was going on was sports editor of the university newspaper, the *Berkeley Gazette*.

On March 25, 1943, Shavenau Glick enlisted in the U.S. Army. The fact that he was a working journalist prior to enlistment got him assigned to public information duty after the required basic training.

Shav was sent to the southwest Pacific to work for a commander he came to dislike. He finally put in a request for a transfer, but his CO, not wanting to lose a good man, tried to block it. Luckily for Shav, MacArthur had a nose for news, and his agents were on constant lookout for talent.

Doug Stokes tells us what Shav had to say about it:

A few weeks after he requested the transfer, his "boss" was pretty hard on him. Shav said, "Then, a day or so later, I was called to the big guy's office and the captain was standing on the front steps red-faced and fuming. He called me over and, without a word, handed me my transfer documents. I looked at the signature, it was one word scrawled across almost the whole bottom of the document: 'MacArthur.'" It was a transfer to Japan and the general's Occupation staff in Tokyo. Shav, who was a bit leaner in his Army days and a good 5'11", told me about walking the streets of that city, his head sticking out of any crowd that he was in. I asked if it wasn't scary to be a young American (in uniform) in a country that we had just brought to their knees. He said that everyone was respectful; that they somehow accepted the situation with great grace.

General MacArthur's "personal public information corps" created much jealousy and rancor among the prideful civilian press corps, competing generals, and ambitious politicians, but it was essential for the success of the Occupation. Early in his 60-year career he had learned the critical importance of public relations for successful leadership.

MacArthur's first assignment, as a young lieutenant, was as an aide to his father, Arthur MacArthur, military governor of the Philippines. Their many tours of the Orient taught him the subtleties of Eastern politics. His six pre-war years as the top military-political figure in the Philippines furthered his education.

Shav during World War II at his desk at MacArthur headquarters in Australia. U.S. Army.

At the outset of the Occupation, besides dealing with the medieval political culture, the British and the Soviets wanted Hirohito's head as a war criminal. The pretentious French, who had cooperated with the Japanese in Vietnam, wanted to participate in the Occupation, as did the USSR. Then there were the hordes seeking to enjoy the spoils of war, another factor to deal with.

After the Japanese capitulation MacArthur's first public relations caper caused a great panic among his staff. The emperor-god Hirohito, whose people would die at his command, had ordered them to accept the defeat with humility. MacArthur's understanding of the Japanese psyche gave him the opportunity for his first grand gesture of the Occupation.

It had been two weeks since the last kamikaze attack on our ships by

18. Shav Glick

fanatics eager to die for their emperor. MacArthur, unprotected, landed at Atsugi Airfield. Without an army to guard him, he was driven the 25 miles to Yokohama along streets lined with thousands of armed Japanese soldiers. It was his personal test of the people's obedience to their emperor. He would save Hirohito from the hangman and use him politically as he might use his artillery in battle.

After the surrender ceremony on the USS *Missouri,* the supreme command of the Allied powers was ensconced in the Dai Ichi building in downtown Tokyo near the imperial palace. Shav Glick sat down at his typewriter and transcribed the supreme commander's orders for the world.

Staff Sergeant Glick was discharged from the Army in 1946. After the war, Shav went home to Pasadena to work on the (now defunct) *Pasadena Post.* Shav added photography to his writing skill and became a combination reporter working on sports. At that time, the *Post* was a morning paper and the *Pasadena Star-News* an evening one, both under the same ownership. Later, the *Post* was discontinued, and Shav stayed with the *Star-News.*

During this time, Shav became a close friend of Joe Mears, who was one of the paper's editors and happened to be my uncle. I lived with him in a house only a few blocks from the *Star-News* offices. In 1946, I was only 12 years old, but even then I was interested in photography after I had received a Brownie box camera for Christmas. Shav was a frequent visitor, sometimes staying for dinner and a few drinks. He would talk with me and give me tips about photography. Little did I know then that we would become lifelong friends when I started racing.

In 1954, Shav went to work for the *Los Angeles Mirror,* still writing about sports. The *Mirror,* however, wouldn't let him take pictures too. During the fifties, he covered races at Santa Barbara, Pomona and Palm Springs, venues where I competed. In 1962, the *Mirror* was discontinued and Shav went with the *Los Angeles Times.* (Both the

Shav at the *Pasadena Star-News,* 1947. Jack McAfee collection.

Shav at Art Evans' home during the 1990s. Photograph by the author.

Times and the *Mirror* were owned by the Chandler family.) In 1969, Shav was appointed the motor sports editor, in which capacity he remained until he retired in 2006 at age 85.

Shav was a frequent visitor to my home when we had parties for my racing compadres. I remember one time he was studying paintings on the wall in my living room. There were two watercolors by his friend, my uncle Joe.

According to an article in the *Times*, "Glick was as likely to be at a sprint car race in Ventura as at the Indianapolis 500. He covered short tracks and super speedways, road racing, drag racing and Midget cars. He was fascinated by unlimited hydroplane racing and, once in the dead of winter, went to La Crosse, Wisconsin, to get a story about stock cars racing on ice."

In the 37 years he covered racing, Shav had won more awards than some of the

Michael Knight (left) and Shav Glick (right) present the James P. Chapman Award for Excellence in Motor Sports Public Relations to Doug Stokes at the 35th Anniversary Auto Racing All-America Team Banquet on January 15, 2005, in Pomona, California.

good drivers who win races. An award was even named after him: the Shav Glick Award. The winners are chosen by a panel of sportswriters and public-relations directors. In 1994 when Shav was inducted into the Motorsports Hall of Fame of America, he thought this honor was the pinnacle of his career. There is a remembrance at his alma mater, Pasadena City College, the Shav Glick Journalism Scholarship. Ed Justice, Jr., has created a Justice Brothers Shav Glick Award, given yearly to recognize significant contributions by a figure in motor sports.

In 1991, Shav's wife of 41 years, Florence, died. Shav died from complications of melanoma on October 20, 2007, at age 87 in his home in Pasadena with his long-time companion, Doris Syme, at his side. Shav was survived by a son, Michael, three grandchildren and two great-grandchildren. He also had a second son, Jeffrey, who died at age 50 of a stroke while working out.

Upon Shav's death, Roger Penske remarked, "I'll always remember him very, very fondly. He was a true friend of mine, a friend of the sporting world and someone with high integrity. I have a lot to thank him for, and so does the entire motor racing industry." Fred Nation at the Indianapolis Motor Speedway called Shav "that rare reporter who combined style, savvy, courtesy and courage to produce the best consistent motorsports reporting of his generation." Shav Glick was universally respected, not only in the newspaper community but also among those involved in the sport he wrote about.

19

Chuck Daigh

Carroll Shelby once remarked, "There are only two people I can think of who could sit down, take a welding torch, build their own chassis, go out to test it and then win races with it. They are Jack Brabham and Chuck Daigh. I put Chuck in the same category as Jack."

Except for the war years, Chuck Daigh was always associated in one way or another with internal combustion engines. At age 15, while still in high school, he ran a Union Oil gas station in Long Beach where he grew up. In his eighth decade he was busy at work preparing a car for a record run at Bonneville. Between those times, he had a legendary career both behind the wheel and wielding a wrench.

Bruce Kessler told me that he thought Chuck was the most under-appreciated racing driver of his time. According to his Sebring teammate, Dan Gurney, "Chuck was not only an excellent engineer, but also he could drive the wheels off a car." Dan went on to say, "When I got into racing, I soon found out who the real heavyweights were. In those days, Chuck was like a god to us."

Chuck's parents moved to Long Beach in 1923, where Charles George Daigh was born on November 29 of that year. His father owned and operated a garage where, according to older brother Harold, they grew up. Both were typical hot rodders. They made a car with a Model A chassis and an Alfa Romeo body. Chuck graduated from Compton High School in 1941.

Along came World War II and Chuck joined up and volunteered to be a paratrooper. He was selected for an elite outfit, the 517th Parachute Infantry Combat Team. He was a member of Company C, First Battalion. The 517th was a small unit that was attached to various divisions to clear out hot spots. They were first blooded in June 1944 clearing the area around Rome, Italy.

On August 15, they were dropped behind German lines in the south of France to open the way for Operation Dragoon/Anvil. During an action near Provence, PFC Daigh captured a German captain's car that contained, among other things, the officer's Luger pistol and some cash. Then he drove to the regimental headquarters to the delight of his teammates. The team spent 90 days there in combat, knocking off roadblocks and hilltops on the way north. PFC Charles G. Daigh was awarded a Bronze Star for valor.

In December, the 517th was attached to the 82nd Airborne Division and moved into Belgium to stem the Bulge. The Bulge was an area where the German Army had attacked and pushed the Allies back, creating a bulge. Chuck's platoon was ambushed in a small village and two were killed. Though wounded, Chuck picked up a Browning Automatic Rifle and sprayed the Germans with gunfire, allowing those in the platoon to escape. Chuck actually fought on the grounds of the Belgian Grand Prix at Spa-Francorchamps. Chuck raced a Scarab in the Belgian Formula One 16 years later on June 19, 1960. The 517th fought its way into Germany before being relieved, having spent 150 combat days in Italy, France, Belgium and Germany, suffering 82 percent casualties.

When the war ended, Chuck was honorably discharged as a corporal. Chuck's brother, Harold, was a Marine combat pilot in the Pacific theater.

Returning to Long Beach, Chuck and Harold built a track roadster and raced it at Carrell Speedway in Gardena. One day Chuck was out practicing when J. C. Agajanian came over and asked Harold who was driving. Harold replied, "Oh, that's Chuck; he's just fooling around." "I don't know about that," J. C. said, "but he just broke the track record!"

In 1952, Benson Ford hired Chuck, Clay Smith and Bill Stroppe to build Lincolns for the Mexican Road Race. Chuck went along as a riding mechanic and navigator. Lincoln won its class in 1952, 1953 and 1954. Sales of Lincolns increased significantly. According to Chuck,

> In the Mexican Road Race days, I worked for Lincoln Mercury. Ford itself was not involved in racing then. In 1956, The Deuce [Henry Ford II] decided that maybe he would dangle his feet in the water a bit, so I left Lincoln Mercury, went to Ford and started the Ford Racing Team based in Long Beach. In those days, the Fords didn't have a large enough gas tank, but the Lincolns did. So we put big Lincoln Continental tanks in all our Fords. We had to. If we didn't, the other guys would beat us with cars that had larger tanks because they could make fewer pit stops for gas.

Chuck's first sports car race as a driver was at Moffett Field in 1953 in Marion Lowe's Frazer Nash. At the Terminal Island race that October, he drove the ex–Don Parkinson Jaguar Special, then owned by Jay Bessemyer. Chuck's Lincoln partner, Bill Stroppe in a Kurtis with a flathead Mercury engine, won the main event. Ken Miles in an R-1 was second, Max Briney in an Allard third and Chuck was fourth in the Jaguar.

In May 1954, Chuck ran a Kurtis with a Lincoln engine for Frank Kurtis at a Willow Springs race. This event saw Chuck's first overall victory, with many more to follow. Interestingly enough, in this victory he beat Stroppe in his Kurtis, as well as Bill Pollack in the Baldwin, Max Balchowsky in his special and John McLaughlin in the Troutman-Barnes Special that Chuck was later to campaign so successfully. At the July Torrey Pines, he in the Kurtis was second overall in the main event behind Ken Miles in the Troutman-Barnes Special. At the fall Santa Barbara race, the finish was reversed with Chuck winning and Miles second.

During the fifties, the SCCA allowed only amateur drivers to compete. A driver would not be allowed to drive after competing in a professional race. In addition to

sports cars, Chuck raced in USAC stock car events. He entered under the name Charles George to avoid SCCA disqualification. On September 15, 1957, he set a track record at the Milwaukee Mile of 90.614 mph.

Starting in 1955 and through 1957, Chuck got the Troutman-Barnes ride driving for Dick and Tom Troutman. Chuck said it was more of a hot rod than a sports car. He won more than his share of races and was always a front-runner. Chuck said,

> When I started racing the Troutman-Barnes, it had an old flathead Ford. Tom Bares built the engine. Both Tom and Dick were working for Kurtis Kraft at the time and were extremely good metal men. Most of the car was built in Barnes's garage because his was larger than the one at Dick's home. Actually, Dick did most of the metal hammering. With the Troutman-Barnes, you had to drive it sideways. It was so short, it went just as fast sideways as straight ahead.

One time Chuck told me about his win at Paramount Ranch in June 1957 when he was on the front row of the main event.

Above: Chuck winning the main event at Paramount Ranch on March 10, 1957. Chuck Daigh collection.

Opposite, top: Chuck Daigh driving the 138 car in the Troutman-Barnes Special at Santa Barbara on March 18, 1956. Bill Murphy follows in the 6 car. *Bottom:* Chuck in the Troutman-Barnes Special at the Pomona Fairgrounds parking lot race on June 24, 1956. Both photographs, Chuck Daigh collection.

Arnie Cane was the starter. He said he didn't start the race; I did. Previously I noticed Arnie would twitch to the right a little bit before he waved the green flag. So when Arnie started to bring his arm up, I left. Lester Nehamkin took a photo of that start. The picture shows Arnie up in the air and all the other cars, but I'm not in it. I had already left.

We used to have a lot of fun with the car. I wasn't very serious about sports car racing then; my business was stock cars. It used to piss off Tom Barnes. One time when I was quite a ways ahead, I pulled into the pits. He asked, "What's wrong?" I replied, "I'll have a cheeseburger and a chocolate malt." He looked at me like I was completely insane. So I took off again.

In 1957, Lance Reventlow asked Troutman and Barnes to build an all-American sports car. The partners wanted to involve Chuck, so he went to work at Warren Olson's shop in Los Angeles where the car was to be constructed. Warren said of Chuck, "He was one of my two most valuable employees; the other being Phil Remington. Chuck would try anything. If something didn't work, it didn't bother him. He would just try something else or do it a different way." Chuck was responsible for the Scarab engine, suspension and brakes. The first Scarab—the Mark I—won its second race at Santa Barbara with Lance at the wheel.

Chuck working on the Reventlow Formula One engine at his shop in Long Beach. Chuck Daigh collection.

19. Chuck Daigh

The first big-time professional road race in Southern California was the U.S. Grand Prix for Sports Cars sponsored by the *Los Angeles Times* in October 1958. Lance had named Chuck his number-one driver and entered him in a Scarab Mark II. Chuck won against very serious competition, including Phil Hill's specially built Ferrari 412S, making a name for the marque. That year, in a Scarab, Chuck won the opener at Meadowdale. At Montgomery he defeated the Cunningham Lister team led by Walt Hansgen and won at Laguna Seca and Nassau.

After the Scarab days, Chuck raced at Sebring three times, winning one with Dan Gurney in a Ferrari Testa Rossa. He also raced in Europe, including Silverstone and Le Mans, usually in a Maserati. During Carroll Shelby's GT-40 effort at Le Mans, Chuck was in charge of carburetion. Even so, the Ford mechanics thought they knew better. Bruce McLaren went out to practice and complained; so, unknown to the factory people, Chuck fixed the problem. Bruce credited both his Le Mans wins in part to Chuck.

During his sports car racing days, Chuck chalked up 17 overall wins, including the Nassau Trophy on July 12, 1958, and the 12 Hours of Sebring on March 21, 1959.

Chuck in the 5 car leading Phil Hill in the 2 car at Riverside on October 12, 1958. Johnny Parsons is in the 181 car. Chuck Daigh collection.

19. Chuck Daigh

Although he competed a few times afterwards, Chuck had pretty much moved out of car racing by the mid-sixties. He started a marine-engine business and had a very successful career in his offshore racer, the *Thunderball*. Chuck not only built the engine but was also at the helm.

In later years, he left Long Beach and moved to Costa Mesa, where he set up shop. A few years ago, I visited Chuck in Costa Mesa. There sat his Bonneville streamliner, up on blocks. It was gorgeous—a work of art! It seemed to me it would be as at home in the Petersen Museum as on the Salt Flats. In 2002 and again in 2003, he prepared the engine for the Formula One Scarab that ran in exhibition at Goodwood. Chuck went along not only as the mechanic but also the driver.

After a brief illness, on Tuesday morning, April 29, 2008, Chuck Daigh passed on. He was 84 years old. He was not only a great driver and designer-mechanic but also a wonderful friend. I miss him. Chuck had married Doris Wingard in 1950 and they were divorced in 1965. They had two children, Denise and Daniel.

Opposite, top: **Starter Arnie Cane flagging the winner, Chuck Daigh, at Paramount Ranch on June 15, 1957. Chuck Daigh collection.** *Bottom, left:* **Chuck in 1958.** *Bottom, right:* **Chuck Daigh at his shop in Long Beach. Both photographs by the author.**

20

Bill Stroppe

Bill Stroppe was among the most versatile and talented of the Southern California racing fraternity, including drivers, fabricators and innovators. He not only raced sports cars but was also involved with stock cars, IndyCars, Midgets and off-road racers. He was undoubtedly one of the greatest engine builders, mechanics and tuners of his time.

Bill was a lifelong resident Long Beach, California. He was born in the city on January 15, 1919, to Ada and Claude Stroppe. He had a sister, Janice, and a brother, Jene. Jene was killed in an automobile accident when Bill was ten years old. His mother never fully recovered from the tragedy.

Bill's parents intended to name him Claude, but somehow the first name was left off his birth certificate. When he entered elementary school, he was told that he was named Claude. But he didn't like the name and said he wanted to be just plain Bill.

His father had a dairy on Signal Hill bordering Long Beach, and young Bill got an early education working on milking machinery and helping maintain the delivery trucks. At an early age, Bill proved to be a genius regarding things mechanical. While still helping his dad at the dairy, Bill got a part-time job at a nearby wrecking yard. His boss let him build his first car out of a wrecked Model T. Then his dad made a deal with a Long Beach service station owner who was going out of business and Bill took over the station at age 14!

Signal Hill, now an incorporated city, stands 365 feet above Long Beach and was originally a site the Indians used for signal fires. It was later used by the Spanish and Americans as a lookout to spot incoming ships to the port at San Pedro. When Bill was two years old, Shell Oil Company's no. 1 oil well gushed to 114 feet in the air, and Signal Hill became one of the most productive oil fields in the world.

The significance for Bill was that he grew up among some of the most innovative people of the 20th century. A Downey farmer, a contemporary of Bill's father, saw an opportunity on Signal Hill.

In 1922, Samuel B. Mosher founded Signal Gasoline Company and took the wet gas that was being flared off at the top of the oil derrick, extracted the gasoline, and sold the dry gas to businesses like the Stroppe Dairy. A Signal Oil facility north of

20. Bill Stroppe

Santa Barbara, California, was shelled by the Japanese submarine I-17 on February 23, 1942. Kozo Nishino, the captain of I-17, had skippered a merchant ship that had loaded oil at that Signal facility, Ellwood Pier, before the war. This attack, so soon after Pearl Harbor, created panic along the West Coast and triggered a false air raid scare the next day in Los Angeles.

Mosher developed Signal into a major gasoline retailer and then diversified, adding to his flock aerospace, airline, and industrial products companies. What a Downey farmer started on Signal Hill is now Honeywell, the $50 billion technology giant. In his early days, he'd probably have dropped into the barbershop adjoining the Stroppe Dairy for a shave.

In 1937, Bill went to Long Beach Polytechnic High School where he played football, majored in auto shop and, most importantly, met his future wife, Helen Tavasti.

At school, Bill spent most of his time in the shop, where he became friends with his teacher, who was also involved with auto racing. Working after school, Stroppe and some other students put together a Midget race car that was driven by Bob Ware at local tracks including Ascot and Gilmore. The car became so successful that, on a summer vacation, they traveled as far as Colorado to race.

Professional race drivers then were supposed to be 21 years old. The youth of the day, with gasoline in their blood, were not to be denied. They stripped early Ford Model T's and A's, hopped-up the engines or installed larger ones, and drove them on the streets or raced them at Muroc Dry Lake. Young Bill not only built his own hot rod but also acquired a 225-class hydroplane, installed a Ford V8, and raced it at Long Beach Marine Stadium and on the Salton Sea.

Bill graduated from high school in 1938 and became fully involved in boat as well as Midget racing. In 1939, he went to work at a Lincoln-Mercury dealership in Long Beach. Thus began Stroppe's association with the Ford Motor Company, which would last a lifetime. His job was new-car preparation. His boss, Art Hall, had Bill help with his boat, a large cabin cruiser.

In early 1941 Stroppe had enlisted in the Naval Air Reserve and spent weekends at Long Beach Naval Air Station, where he was trained in aircraft maintenance. Long Beach was home port for the Pacific Fleet battleships until they were moved to Pearl Harbor in 1940. When the Japanese attacked on December 7, 1941, the reserves were called to active duty, and the Naval Air Station became a training post and was moved to a new base at Los Alamitos. In the spring of 1942, Bill got a weekend pass and he and Helen drove to Yuma, Arizona, and were married on March 22.

Bill got his chance to see action when he went to sea aboard the USS *Casco*, a seaplane tender. A seaplane tender acted as a seagoing airport for float planes and flying boats. The ship was assigned to service a seaplane squadron and carried bombs, torpedoes, spare parts and 80,000 gallons of aviation gasoline. That presented a choice target for Japanese pilots.

From 1942 to 1943, the *Casco* operated in Aleutian waters off Alaska. It was torpedoed August 30, 1942, by the Japanese sub RO-61, killing 5 men and wounding 20. The *Casco* didn't sink, and after stateside repairs, she returned to the Aleutians in

March 1943 to cover the expulsion of the Japanese from Attu and Kiska Islands and then headed south to battles in the South Pacific.

Bill's early experience with machinery and fabrication made him an invaluable member of the *Casco*'s crew. While at sea, in rough waters, he repaired an OS2U Kingfisher's engine while it hung off the ship's stern crane. He fabricated a metal ramp to replace a wooden one that could splinter dangerously if hit with shellfire. Bill also invented a unique fueling device and procedure that won him a Presidential Citation and became standard practice for the fleet.

The captain was concerned that his ship could be struck by Japanese kamikaze pilots. He asked aircraft machinist's mate Bill Stroppe for a suggestion. The ship had aboard some floating smoke bombs that were used by downed pilots to signal their location. Bill devised a plan to disperse these smoke bombs around the ship to provide a smoke screen and hide it from the enemy. The acrid smoke was a problem for the crew, so back to the drawing board. Bill approached the job as if he were building a race car and fabricated a Rube Goldberg device that had numerous pipes, ports and an oil-burning boiler. It was used for the duration of the war.

The *Casco* sailed for the Marshall Islands in February 1944 to provide critical seaplane coverage of our central Pacific operations. She also supplied fuel for the motor torpedo (PT) boats that were powered by the Packard Merlin aircraft engine.

While she was standing offshore from Saipan at the end of 1944 fueling, a four-engined flying boat, a Consolidated PB2Y Coronado, crashed into the *Casco*. Stroppe was injured and thrown into the sea. A rescue boat was quickly launched, and the sailors pulled Bill aboard. Then he was transferred to the Navy hospital ship, *USS Samaritan* (AH10). When he was partially recovered, but still in pain, he returned to the *Casco* for the Philippine and Okinawa campaigns. He was honorably discharged on February 2, 1946.

At the end of a highly meritorious tour of duty defending his country, Bill Stroppe returned to his roots in Long Beach. He built and campaigned a new Kurtis Midget driven by an outstanding selection of future champions and Indy 500 winners: Johnny Mantz, Troy Ruttman, and Bill Vukovich were among them. Stroppe also multi-tasked, returning to boat racing with his own 135-hydroplane and a 225-hydro owned by a local car dealer. During this era, some of the Long Beach boat boys shook up Europe by beating European-engined boats with a Cracker Box class using a hopped-up Ford V8 engine.

Come the 1950s, Bill himself saddled up and started racing sports cars. He began with an MGTC in which he installed a Ford V8–60 engine and shared driving with Phil Hill. His first race was at the California Sports Car Club's initial wheel-to-wheel event at the Carrell Speedway, a dirt oval on the outskirts of Los Angeles. Stroppe drove his MG V8 Special there on July 28, 1951, to a third overall. Bill returned to Carrell Speedway on June 21, 1952, where he won overall.

Bill's first sports car road race was an SCCA event at Reno, Nevada, on September 21, 1951. Again in the MG, he was fifth overall. At Palm Springs the next weekend, he was second overall and first in class. After two more races in the MG, he turned the

20. Bill Stroppe

Bill Stroppe drove the Kurtis at Carrell Speedway near Los Angeles on January 18, 1953. He won the Trophy Dash. Photograph by Dave Friedman.

car, the famous 2Jr, over to Phil Hill, who began his climb to becoming a world champion in it.

When Frank Kurtis decided to build an American sports car, Bill bought the very first short-wheelbase 500S and ran it at Phoenix, Stockton, Chino, Seafair, Moffett Field and Santa Barbara, all of which he won overall, much to the chagrin of the purists in Ferraris, Maseratis and Jaguars. In later years, Bill drove a beautifully restored Kurtis 500S at a number of vintage events, including the revised La Carrera Classic in 1986. The Classic was an Art Evans Vintage Racing project that ran from Ensenada on the Pacific Ocean 120 miles up over the 5,000-foot mountain range and down to San Felipe on the Sea of Cortez. It was a real test for a vintage sports car running on questionable pavement.

Even though Bill's business revolved around motor racing, racing sports cars was just a hobby for him. He had promised Art Hall before the war that he would be back, and so he returned to his job at the Hall Lincoln-Mercury agency in Long Beach. With Hall's interest in boats, Bill got involved with boat racing again. He built a boat named the *Hellcat* and raced it in the 135- and 225-cubic-inch classes at the Long Beach Marine Stadium and other venues. Art Hall decided to run his boat, the *Miss Art Hall*, at the 1947 Henry Ford Memorial Regatta in Detroit, Michigan. The boat had a Ford engine that needed Stroppe's massaging. After Bill's magic touch, the boat was the fastest qualifier in the 225 class. Bill drove the boat and won the race, much to the delight of Ford. The 225 and 135 classes matched the Ford V8 and V8–60 engine sizes. For most of his career, Bill was involved in one way or another with the Ford Motor Company. Benson Ford, Jr., then head of the Lincoln-Mercury Division, and Bill became lifelong friends. The friendship deepened Bill's involvement with Mercury.

In 1950, with Clay Smith driving and Stroppe navigating, they entered and won the Mobilgas Economy Run in a Mercury Monterey. Beforehand, Bill had torn down the engine and blueprinted it: that means checking every dimension, weight and balance, and correcting them to exact design specifications. (This practice is now common to showroom stock and production car racing. Professional engine builders even get access to factory part bins to search for the most perfect stock part.) The next year, they failed to win the sweepstakes but did take their class win. They won the sweepstakes again in 1952.

Stroppe (left) with Parnelli Jones. They were totally successful in off-road racing. Photograph by Dave Friedman.

20. Bill Stroppe

Above: Bill Stroppe at his shop in Long Beach in 1990. Photograph by the author.
Right: In 1941, Bill Stroppe enlisted in the U.S. Naval Reserve at the Naval Station in Long Beach. Stroppe collection.

The Mexican government, in 1950, established a race to mark the opening of the paved road from the American border at El Paso south to Guatemala. It was called the Carrera Panamericana (the Pan American Road Race). The first race ran from Guatemala north to Ciudad Juarez. With Lincoln-Mercury dealer Bob Estes as a sponsor, Stroppe and his partner, Clay Smith, prepared the Lincoln Capris that won their class in the race three consecutive years. In 1952 it was Chuck Stevenson–Clay Smith first and Johnny Mantz–Bill Stroppe second. In 1953 Stevenson-Smith repeated their win with Walt Faulkner–Chuck Daigh second and Mantz-Stroppe fourth. The last Carrera in 1954 saw Ray Crawford–Davalos Iglesias winning, with Faulkner-Hainley second.

In 1956, Ford decided that Bill Stroppe would head their onslaught on American stock car racing using Mercurys. Drivers Troy Ruttman, Sam Hanks and Jimmy Bryan ran the beach at Daytona and won a number of races all over the country. Sam won the race and set a record at Paramount Ranch in California.

In 1964 Stroppe and Mercury challenged the USAC Stock Car Circuit with Parnelli Jones driving. They contested 15 dirt ovals, plus Pikes Peak. They won 7 ovals, plus the Peak and the Championship.

Off-road racing had become a big-time sport, and in 1968, Stroppe partnered with Parnelli Jones, developing the Ford Bronco, which won just about everything there was to win. According to Parnelli, "For a long time, I was paired up with Bill Stroppe, who from the early 1950s had been a part of Ford's racing program. Bill was not only

Above: Vintage Racing. Bill Stroppe raced his Kurtis in the Vintage Races at Laguna Seca Raceway near Monterey, California, in 1984. Photograph by the author. *Right:* Bill Stroppe in his twenties. Stroppe collection.

a gentleman, but also a *gentle man*, a pleasant person to be around. Every car that came from Stroppe's shop was *immaculate*. No dirt, no dents, everything top-shelf." In 1978 Bill Stroppe was inducted into the Off-Road Motorsports Hall of Fame.

An example of the engineering problems that required Stroppe's genius was suspension travel. On a glass-smooth course, no spring is needed. A go-kart is an example. The first off-roaders might have six inches of wheel travel. Shops like Bill's developed suspension elements that allowed over 30 inches of movement in order to absorb the most severe bumps at over 100 mph.

In later years, Stroppe became involved in a number of events. He was even a part of an attempt to set the hot-air balloon transcontinental record! Bill also built a 1909 Model T Ford for the 1983 Historic Auto Races at Monterey.

Bill Stroppe died November 7, 1995, at age 76 after surgery resulting from a fall. A shop called Bill Stroppe & Son was operated by his son, Willie, in Paramount, California. It closed in 2008 after the economic problems that affected the automotive world. Willie and his wife, Debbie, live in North Long Beach, California. Bill's daughter, Luanne and her husband, Burdett Hallett, reside in Huntington Harbour, California. Bill's beloved wife, Helen, passed away on March 19, 2016, at the age of 94.

21

Pete Lovely

Gerard Carlton Lovely was born on April 11, 1926, in Livingston, Montana, to Gerard and Mildred Lovely. We knew him as Pete (not Peter!). When she was pregnant, his ordinarily thin mother looked as if she would have twins. His dad said if they were girls, they would be named Kate and Duplicate; if boys, Pete and Repeat. The result turned out not to be twins, just one boy.

His father was a rancher who supplied horses to pull plows. Along came tractors and then the Depression and the ranch went broke. Then the family moved to Seattle, Washington.

Pete's life is an example of the making of the Greatest Generation. His first five years were spent on a horse ranch where neighbors were converting from horses to tractors and trucks. Imagine the conversations and arguments a child would be exposed to. While Tom Mix and William S. Hart were loving their horses on the silver screen, the kids were enthralled by the huge Holt Brothers diesel-powered crawler tractors. Holt Brothers of Sacramento, California, moved to Peoria, Illinois, and became the Caterpillar Tractor Company. Analogous to those times would be today's children leaping far ahead of their parents deep into the computer world.

Pete's teenage years were spent in a rural community, Livingston, where his dad was the sheriff. Small towns usually provide youth more opportunity to be aware of adult activities, such as the stories and arguments that could be heard at the local barbershop.

Then there was the big jump when the family moved to Seattle, where he completed high school while his dad worked at Boeing Aircraft on the B-29 that dropped the atom bomb. Pete had attended Park County High School in Livingston, then transferred to Garfield High School in Seattle, Washington, in 1943.

So Pete Lovely grew up in an era where men were adapting engines and electric motors to machines that had been hand-, horse-, or water-powered. For instance, an "icebox" had a metal-lined box with a lid on top of the food storage compartment. A 50-pound block of ice went into the metal box. General Electric took the lid and attached cooling coils to the bottom and an electric-motor-driven condenser to the top. Such were the innovations of the first half of the 20th century.

After high school graduation at age 18 on July 29, 1944, he entered military service. His mechanical aptitude got him into the Army Air Corps Aviation Mechanics School. Military mechanics, especially on aircraft, requires extreme discipline. The training served Pete well in his future endeavors.

Discharged in 1946, his skill led to a job at North American Aviation in El Segundo, California. North American had produced the AT-6, B-25, P-51 and was working on the F-86 and the B-47.

At North American he worked on the new F-86 swept-wing jet fighters. James Howard "Dutch" Kindelberger, head of North American Aviation, had acquired the plans of the German Messerschmitt 262 and built our first competitive jet fighter. While working at North American, Pete was exposed to the Southern California car culture.

Post-war auto production and war-surplus vehicles had relegated older cars to the scrap heap. The youth of the time, with little money, took the lightweight old cars and installed larger motors. Some were surplus Cadillac tank engines, but most were Ford or Mercury V8s. The hot rods were the American sports cars of the 1940s. The post-war racing craze had taken hold, and the California Roadster Association started racing the hot rods, along with the Midgets, on dirt ovals. There were races seven nights a week, plus Saturday and Sunday afternoons.

As a new civilian, Pete used his mustering-out pay to buy a 1932 Ford roadster and install in it a Ford V8 truck engine. The aircraft plants were a great source for race car hardware. He campaigned it at local oval tracks from 1947 to 1950. While still racing the roadster, he acquired an MGTC and became interested in road racing. Then he sold the TC and bought a Renault 4CV and entered it in a road race at Ft. Lewis, just south of Tacoma, Washington. The Renault 4CV was a Volkswagen bug competitor. It was very low, and it had a four-cylinder water-cooled rear engine. It drove like a go-kart. He failed to win with it, so he traded the Renault for an XK120 Jaguar, returned to Ft. Lewis the following weekend and placed first overall. Pete raced the Jaguar until 1954, when he built his first special, a VW-Porsche. He didn't have a trailer, so he drove the car from his home in Seattle down to San Francisco and placed second at Golden Gate Park.

In 1954, Pete started his own VW dealership, bought a Cooper Streamliner record car and installed a Porsche engine. It became the famous Pooper in which he won the 1955 F-modified SCCA National Championship.

Colin Chapman, the Lotus designer said, "Add horsepower, you increase straight-line speed; reduce weight and you increase speed everywhere." Chapman was prone to overdo it and Lotus cars sometimes broke. Pete was the first to use a Cooper with a Porsche engine in his Pooper. Ken Miles followed, but his effort was scotched by the Porsche factory. Then in 1961, Jack Brabham and Bruce McLaren finished first and second in the 1961 Los Angeles Times Grand Prix in Coopers; Roger Penske won the 1962 race with his lightweight Cooper Zerex Special; Carroll Shelby's King Cobra, a Cooper Monaco with Ford V8 in the back, won in 1963 with Dave MacDonald driving and again in 1964 with Parnelli Jones driving.

Pete entered his Pooper in the 1956 Pebble Beach event. Some years ago he told me,

Pete Lovely in his VW-Porsche Special leading Al Coppel in his Osca MT4 at the 1954 Golden Gate. Pete and Al engaged in a race-long duel, trading places a number of times. Pete finished second and Al third. Lovely collection.

> In 1955, I bought a Streamliner from John Cooper. It was British Racing Green and gorgeous. I installed a Porsche Super engine and a VW gearbox. At Pebble, there was a whole bunch of Porsche Spyders, but at only 920 pounds, my Pooper was a lot lighter. [The Porsche 550 weighed in at 1,220 pounds.] Early on, I was either second or in the lead when, coming out of Turn Three, the throttle pedal went all the way to the floor and the engine went to idle. So I pulled over to see what had gone wrong. It was apparent the cable that connected the pedal to the carburetors had come undone. I realized I couldn't fix it on the course. So I got in the car, reached back with my left hand, worked the throttle and got back up to speed. The only problem was that when I shifted, I had to momentarily let go of the wheel. So I would wait until a straight stretch to shift. With the four-speed VW box, I could shift rapidly. I knew that there wasn't anything I could do back in the pits to fix it in less than 30 minutes, so I decided to keep going. I ended up fourth overall!

In 1957, Pete joined the GMC factory team at Sebring driving an SR2 Corvette. Some time afterwards, he told me his remembrances:

> About two weeks before the race, John Fitch called me on the phone and said he needed another driver. He had called me because of the successes I had had driving the Pooper. I had

Top: Pete and his first wife, Patricia, after he won the semi-main for modified cars under 1500cc at the Grand Central Sports Car Races (airport in Glendale, California) in his Pooper on November 13, 1955. Pete and Patricia had four children: Chris, Linda, Laurie and Lisa. Lovely collection. *Bottom:* Pete took his famous Pooper to the Glendale race on November 13, 1955, on his way to an SCCA National Championship.

Jack McAfee followed by Pete at the November 4, 1956, race at Palm Springs. Lovely collection.

won the SCCA National Championship again in 1956 in my class, F-Modified. I replied, "Well yeah, I can come, no problem." After the race started and just as it was getting dark, my teammate, Paul O'Shea, was going down the Warehouse Straight and he put the brakes on, but they didn't work. So he went straight off into a sandy berm that was about four feet high. When he hit the berm, he went right through it. So he drove around slowly and came back to the pits. I got in the car and put on my open-face helmet. I drove to the end of the pit lane and was waved out. When I accelerated, all of a sudden, I was almost blinded. When Paul had gone through the berm, a lot of sand got on the floorboard. It blew up under my helmet. So I came back in and, while I was trying to get the sand out of my eyes, the mechanics got a vacuum cleaner and cleaned it all out. We lost a lot of time what with all those goofy things going wrong, and we ended up 16th or something like that.

John Fitch told me, "Pete Lovely was one of my stalwart drivers. I respected his talent for top speed with no mistakes—and he delivered."

On November 10, 1957, the first race meet was held at the new Laguna Seca Course at Fort Ord, California. Pete Lovely drove a two-liter Ferrari Testa Rossa. He was up against some serious competition, including Carroll Shelby. Towards the end of the race, Pete was behind the leader, John Von Neumann in a three-liter Ferrari. Pete remembered, "I came up right behind him. At Turn 11, I was in first gear and I squirted ahead of him when I caught second gear. John had missed his shift. He just didn't get it in second gear." So Pete Lovely won the very first main event at Laguna Seca.

21. Pete Lovely

Pete in his Ferrari won the first race at Laguna Seca on November 4, 1957. Lovely collection.

In 1957 Pete had bought and campaigned a Lotus MK VIII. Wanting to upgrade, he flew to England to visit the Lotus factory. His charm and talent impressed Colin Chapman and he was offered a drive in a Lotus 15 at Le Mans in 1958 with Jay Chamberlain. They crashed out after eight hours. He got a second chance at the Rheims 12-Hour Race where, driving with Innes Ireland, they won their class. In 1959 Pete and Jay Chamberlain drove a Lotus Elite at the 12 Hours of Sebring.

Pete's record was such that he was invited to join Team Lotus in 1959. When he arrived in Europe, he found that he was expected to survive on prize money. That year's Lotus wasn't very reliable, so when the money he had brought with him ran out, he returned home.

The following year, on March 26, 1960, Pete and Jack Nethercutt placed third overall at the 12 Hours of Sebring race even though they spent 39 minutes in the pits with a split fuel tank. Then on April 3, 1960, Pete finished third at the Los Angeles Examiner Grand Prix at Riverside in Nethercutt's Ferrari.

The 1960 U.S. Formula One Grand Prix was run at Riverside Raceway on November 20, 1960. Pete had to have a go at it, and he stuffed a 2.5-liter Ferrari engine that he bought from John Von Neumann into a Cooper and had at it. He and his elderly

Pete drove a factory Corvette at the 1957 12 Hours of Sebring. Lovely collection.

machine lost an extra four minutes in the pits and finished six laps behind the winner, Stirling Moss.

During the 1960s Pete took an eight-year hiatus from racing to tend to family matters and to grow his VW dealership. By 1969, his blood was up again, and he revisited his Formula One dream. He purchased the Lotus 49B in which Graham Hill had supposedly won the previous year's Monaco Grand Prix. Pete finished seventh at the Canadian and ninth at the Mexican Grand Prix.

The Lotus Pete bought was supposed to be 49B-11 but it appeared that, as is usual with race cars, there had been a lot of parts swapping and maybe some number changes. It seems the Lotus was actually the 49B-2 that had won the first race for the Cosworth DFV-V8 at the Belgian Grand Prix at Spa with Jimmy Clark driving. The car was sold years later to Chris MacAllister who crashed it at Monaco in a vintage race.

In 1985 when I ran the vintage races at Palm Springs, I called Pete and asked him to join us, so he loaded his Lotus on his VW pickup and started to drive from Tacoma. On the way, he got stuck in a snowstorm. Somehow, he made his way to an airport and arrived on time. So I got him a ride in a borrowed Lotus and he made the race! In more recent times, Pete added a vintage race car restoration shop to his dealership. Then he sold the dealership and started traveling all over the world entering historic events. In 1999 and again in 2000, Pete and his wife, Nevele, were invited to Australia for the Race of Legends.

He was a consistent entrant at the Monterey Historics, often running his 49B in the Formula One race. He had a large transporter complete with kitchen and chef. I was fortunate to be asked to partake of the wonderful paddock food and drink as well as enjoy the companionship.

I was saddened to learn that Pete Lovely died on May 15, 2011. He was a wonderful friend and a great competitor. I understand that he passed on peacefully with two of his daughters at his side. Pete's beloved wife, Nevele, had died in 2008. Some friends remarked to me that he never really recovered from losing her. Nevele was a sweetheart, and she always told people, "You can't forget my name or the spelling because it's eleven backwards."

Pete in the paddock at Laguna Seca during the 1992 Monterey Historics. Photograph by the author.

22

Max Balchowsky

Max Balchowsky was an outlier. Not a rebel or a hermit but an individual, in the best sense. With limited resources he created purpose-focused machines. He grew up during the Great Depression in the poorest of the coal mining country. He spent World War II on three continents, North America, Europe, and then Asia. After a youth spent in meager circumstances, he wrenched himself a place in the glamour capital of the world, Hollywood, which was situated in what was a utopian wonderland during his time in its history.

Max acclimated himself to this unbelievable change in the environment without losing his creative individuality and, with very limited resources, achieved greatness in his own way. When he died, he had garnered international acclaim in his chosen field, great respect in the movie industry, and most important, the love of everyone who knew him.

Max Balchowsky, like many people of accomplishment, was not a physically imposing figure or an aggressive personality. By his appearance you might downplay the intellect of this short, dark man in coveralls. But ask him a question and it was like opening an encyclopedia: ask about tire pressure and he could go all the way to telling you how to grow a rubber tree.

Max never flaunted his knowledge or his success. If he happened by when you had a problem, he would quietly try to help. If you were pushing your broken car, you might look back and see Max leaning in to help. He eschewed hype when it came to his cars. When the newspaper boys were lusting after big horsepower numbers, Max might deduct a hundred or so, and tell them about the importance of torque. Max won his races by reworking American engines and homebuilt race cars. His collection of sows' ears didn't become silk purses; they were fashioned into durable wallets.

Max Ernest Balchowsky was born on January 15, 1924, in Fairmont, West Virginia, coal country 90 miles south of Pittsburgh on the Monongahela River. His father had died young. At age 16, Max quit high school and took on gigs repairing bicycles or driving cars, trucks, buses, and even tractors to help his family.

On April 10, 1943, 19-year-old Max enlisted in the U.S. Army Air Corps. After basic training he was sent to gunnery school and then, because of his size, he was assigned the worst job on an airplane; ball turret gunner on a Consolidated B-24. The ball turret is a metal and plexiglass sphere mounted on the underside of the B-24, and it contains two .50-caliber machine guns and a small man in a fetal position. To enter the turret the guns had to be lowered to the down position. There was no room for a parachute. Bail-out procedure was to move the guns to the down position, climb into the airplane, don your parachute and jump with the waist gunners. If the plane's electrical system had been shot out, a waist gunner had to hand crank the turret into position for his escape.

Unluckily Max had to bail out of a flak-damaged plane over Italy. Luckily for Max and the world, though, he was only injured. He landed in friendly territory and survived. When Max was again fit for duty, he was sent to the far side of the world, the China-Burma-India theater of operations. Though much less publicized than Europe, there was great intrigue with dire portent for America's future brewing in that arena.

Not only were Indians clamoring for independence from England, several Chinese factions were vying for power. Vietnamese factions, Ho Chi Minh's Viet Minh the foremost of them, were trying to boot the French in accord with Roosevelt's, and a reluctant Churchill's, 1941 Atlantic Charter Declaration.

Logistics and transport in the mountainous and jungled area were a nightmare. The B-24 was not only a bomber but also an occasional transport. The B-24s supported "Vinegar Joe" Stillwell's campaign in Burma. They dropped bombs on the Japanese and dropped supplies to Merrill's Marauders and Orde Wingate's Chindits who were fighting in the jungle behind Japanese lines. They also flew dangerous radar-directed low-level night missions attacking shipping in the Gulf of Tonkin off the coast of Vietnam.

Classified secret until recently, the OSS Dixie Mission parachuted their Deer Team into North Vietnam and, working with Ho's Viet Minh, established radio intelligence stations and rescued 574 downed airmen. They instructed the Viet Minh in the use of modern weapons and tactics. OSS Colonel Archimedes Patti commanded the Vietnam operations from Kunming, China. The Vichy French had allowed the imperial Japanese forces to occupy Vietnam in 1940 and were not helpful to Allied interests in the area. Max's flight fatigues had identifying messages in several Asian languages and in French. Being a lifelong learner, he had picked up a Japanese-English translation book that was left on his plane and was attempting to teach himself Japanese. When caught with the book, he was brought up on charges and faced a court-martial. Unbeknownst to Max, the book was a part of an OSS communications operation code kit that was highly classified. People dealing with our codes had a crypto clearance, which was higher than top secret. In fact, a dozen enlisted men with crypto clearance were evacuated from Corregidor in 1942 along with General MacArthur and his aides. Court-martial proceedings were dropped when it was noted the book was not marked "secret" and by itself had no significance. Max was allowed to keep the book.

When Max was discharged from the Air Corps, he joined his brother, Caspar, in California, where they operated a gas station and transmission repair shop in South Gate. Always eager to learn, he studied watchmaking in Glendale on the G.I. Bill. The kid from the West Virginia coal mines had landed in the middle of the most concentrated auto racing environment in the country. Frank Kurtis in Glendale and Joel Thorne in Burbank built Indianapolis 500 winners. Art Sparks, the genius mechanic, had taught at Glendale High School. Glendale's hot rod club, the Sidewinders, was number one in the Southern California Timing Association, the group that organized time trials on the dry lakes. Max and Caspar became dedicated hot rodders. During the 1940s, before dragstrips and with a lot of open space, street racing was common in the Los Angeles area.

At Culver City in 1945, the street racers met up at Pic's Drive-In and went off down Washington Place, west of Sepulveda Boulevard. Washington Place was a new four-lane street through a residential area that was undeveloped because of the Depression and then the war. East of Sepulveda Boulevard, on Washington Place, was the speed shop of Karl and Veda Orr and Sandy Belond's muffler shop. Belond had sponsored Sam Hanks's 1957 Indy winner. When the area developed, and law enforcement got too hot, the action moved all the way out to the north San Fernando Valley. Sepulveda Boulevard at San Fernando Mission Road rose abruptly several hundred feet and then ran level north for three miles to a junction with Highway 99. Sepulveda was three-lane concrete with no side streets. It passed between the Van Norman Lakes that were part of the Mulholland water project. At the intersection with 99 there was a Chevron station, a restaurant, and large parking lot, creating a perfect staging area for the midnight Wednesday drag races. On a good night it was like an organized auto show. The road is now the 405 freeway and at mid-point to the east of the 405 is Sylmar, the location of the Nethercutt Auto Museum.

While at school in Glendale, Max had met Ina Wilson; watchmaking didn't last, but Ina became his lifelong partner. She was born in Los Angeles on October 12, 1931. When Ina graduated high school in 1949, she and Max were married. Ina's father owned a garage, and she had grown up changing spark plugs instead of diapers and welding seams instead of sewing them.

In 1950, sports cars and road racing flooded into Southern California like grunion on a rising tide. Max and Ina took a weekend drive up Highway 395 past the desert dry lakes, through the ski resorts and on to Reno, Nevada, where there was a road race scheduled. They were delivering a station wagon in which they had installed a Cadillac V8 for Bill Harrah, the casino owner. Reno was the gambling and divorce capital in 1950 before Bugsy Segal and the mob took an interest in Las Vegas and built the Flamingo Hotel and Casino. At the race, Max talked Bill Harrah into letting him drive his XK120 Jaguar in the novice race. Max was hooked. The weekend was an SCCA National event, and Bill Pollack won the main race in Tom Carstens's J2 Cad Allard.

Max and Ina opened their own shop in 1952, and she was a full partner, in the office and on the wrenches. She was a pro welder. Their shop, Hollywood Motors, was at 4905 Hollywood Boulevard, near Vermont. Just west of them on the boulevard was Competition Body Shop run by George and Walter who manned the California Sports Car Club's tow truck. George was the painter and the famous Von Dutch did the pinstripes. Farther west on the boulevard, Reginald Denny, British actor and poor man's

22. Max Balchowsky

Max Balchowsky drove the Bu-Ford Special at Torrey Pines on December 14, 1952. It was a 1932 Ford Roadster with a highly-modified Buick engine. Max Balchowsky collection.

Ronald Colman, had a model airplane shop. He was a pioneer in radio-control flight, founding Radio Plane Corporation, which built target drones and, after the war, was sold to Northrop. He is the father of today's drones.

Unlike the huge Hollywood egos with their faces and logos on billboards, the big white Balchowsky garage on Hollywood Boulevard never had a sign. Inside, it was classic 1920s, including a large drive-over grease pit in lieu of a hydraulic lift. Max's trademark was his coveralls. In the shop they were white twill with a shop rag dangling from the back pocket. But he also had a wardrobe of "go to town" coveralls tailored in finer fabric. Marlon Brando and James Dean turned Hollywood on to denim; Max wore gabardine coveralls. He cut a fine figure at many social events. Like an artist's atelier or an author's writing den, Max had bins and shelves stacked with auto parts of every description, new and recycled, but the floor was always spotless.

Max and his wife, Ina, always worked together. And both of them drove the cars. This photograph was taken at their shop in Los Angeles in 1957. Max Balchowsky collection.

As the years went by, Hollywood Motors became a hangout for real-world actors who appreciated machinery. Steve McQueen, a close friend of Max, had a classic gearhead line in the movie *The Sand Pebbles*. In his role as a Navy machinist's mate reporting for duty on an old gunboat on the Yangtze River in China, he goes below, and in a tender voice, while leaning on a steam valve, says, "Hello engine, I'm Jake Holman." That line expressed Max's feelings for his machines.

McQueen, James Dean, James Coburn, and Elvis Presley were a few of the stars he worked with. Max's real bread and butter in the motion picture industry was technical preparation and stunt work. His very good friend Carey Loftin was the godfather of car stunts. Max set up the cars for McQueen's legendary chase through the streets of San Francisco in the movie *Bullitt*. Max's list of movie credits is longer than his race credits. Haskell Wexler, the Oscar-winning cinematographer, became the sponsor of Max's Old Yeller III, IV and V.

Max in Old Yeller at the 1956 Santa Barbara Airport races. Max Balchowsky collection.

Max's dual career, making movies and road racing, began on December 14, 1952, at Torrey Pines near San Diego, a race on an abandoned Army base. He drove Fred Vogel's Ford Special and drove the car again at Reno in October 1953.

With a wife and a new business, Max settled into his lifework making a living modifying and racing cars. He and Ina bought a '32 Ford roadster with a war-surplus Cadillac tank engine. They exchanged the Caddy for a Buick and called it the Bu-Ford Special. Max raced the Bu-Ford eight times in 1954, and Ina won the ladies' race at the SCCA National at March Air Force Base on November 7. On the tight Pebble Beach

From his beginnings with sports cars, Max was an expert in getting the most out of the Buick engines in the Old Yellers. This photograph was taken at his and Ina's shop in Los Angeles in 1954. Max Balchowsky collection.

road course through the pine trees, Max muscled the '32 roadster to an eighth place in the SCCA National held there on April 17, 1955. Another SCCA National held in Bakersfield on May 1 was the last race for the Bu-Ford. There was a new girl in town, Dorothy Deen's beautiful Doretti.

The Doretti has a history of its own. Max's involvement was one of the first of many people's attempts to produce a Shelby Cobra–type car. Swallow Coachbuilding was an English company that built motorcycle sidecars. Arthur Andersen and his daughter, Dorothy Deen, were Southern California business people, owners of Cal Sales. They wanted to build an upscale Triumph TR2-type sports car for the American market. Doretti was Dorothy's name Italianized.

Father and daughter worked out a deal with Swallow and Standard Triumph to distribute the Doretti in the western United States. The Doretti was larger and stronger than the TR2 but used the Triumph's engine and running gear. Max's idea was to put a Buick V8 in the sturdy little car and create a big-bore winner. Max got one and stuffed the Buick in it and took it to the races. He was able to grab third place at the SCCA National at the Grand Central Airport in Glendale on November 13, 1955. Grand Central was Los Angeles' main airport until 1938 and home base for Howard Hughes and other aviation pioneers. It's now a business park and home to some of Disney Studios' operations. The roadblock to success for the Doretti was limited capital. Swallow had only 18 employees and could produce only one car a day. They had to shut down after only 275 cars were built. So Max's attempt to beat Carroll Shelby to the draw was nipped in the bud. Max raced the Doretti 11 times in 1955 and 1956. The third place at Glendale was his best finish. His last race in the Doretti was on May 20, 1956, at Bakersfield.

In January of 1956 he reconnected with his Bu-Ford and co-drove the Torrey Pines six-hour race with Eric Hauser. The car was entered as the Powell Bu-Ford Special by Gladys Powell. Thus began the story of Old Yeller. At this race meet, Margaret Pritchard, driving the Morgensen Special, crashed and was killed. Max and Eric Hauser bought the wrecked car, stuck a Buick engine in it, and began its development. The car had many names, including Outhauser, before it was painted yellow and became the legendary Old Yeller MKI on June 29, 1958, at Riverside.

During the 1950s there were numerous attempts to build a winning all-American sports racing car. They ranged from Jay Chamberlain's Ford Model T with a flathead V8 engine, the Eliminator that was campaigned by Frank "Duffy" Livingstone, the father of go-karting, to the million-dollar Scarab Chevy manufactured by Lance Reventlow. In between were Kurtis Cadillacs, Kurtis Buicks, a Kurtis with Jaguar running gear and a Chrysler hemi V8. There was Evans Industries' Devin SS Chevy, and all the Devin-bodied specials. Almost every make of sports car ended up with a small block Chevy in it. One was even squeezed into a VW, but never into a Porsche. Max, who chalked out the frame on the garage floor, built a special with a Chevy engine for Dave MacDonald, the hot Corvette driver.

Max and Ina persevered with the job of perfecting the Morgensen Special to become Old Yeller I. Eric Hauser, driving in the rain, wearing his candy-striped long-sleeve polo shirt, finally won the main events at Santa Barbara on May 18 and 19, 1957. The partnership was not a happy one as Max and Eric were worlds apart in terms of personality. Eric took the body and chassis, Max took the engine and transmission, and they had a parting of the ways. Max and Ina started from scratch and built the true legend, Old Yeller II, the junkyard dog that ate Ferraris. It debuted at Riverside on October 11, 1959. Not only was it American, it was recycled American. Almost every top West Coast driver of the era led or won a race driving Old Yeller II. The short list includes Dan Gurney, Carroll Shelby, Bob Bondurant, Ronnie Bucknam, Bill Krause, Bob Drake, Paul O'Shea, and of course, Max Balchowsky himself.

Even with the publicity garnered at the time for beating the expensive pedigreed thoroughbreds, and with the current nostalgic acclaim, the Balchowskys' accomplishment is underrated. Acknowledgment of their achievement in the record books was hampered by poor reliability. Max's car was usually in the top three places in every race it finished; it was a leader in every race it entered. It was lauded as the best-handling and easiest-to-drive car of its time by top drivers, including Dan Gurney. The amazing thing is that this car was put together by a mom and pop operation out of recycled production parts at minimum cost. It competed against million-dollar operations with large teams, plush facilities and fully equipped transporters. In the true spirit of the sports car, Max and Ina would drive Old Yeller to the track. John Edgar's 4.5 Maserati cost $20,000 in 1957. An MGA listed at $2,500, which is more than Old Yeller II cost to build. In fact, a Ferrari cylinder head cost more than Max's car. Not having the manpower or the finances, and having to rely on production parts, Max

Carroll Shelby drove Max's Old Yeller in July 1960 at Road America. Shelby led the race from the start and was gaining on the second-place car when the transmission let go and he was robbed of a sure win. Shelby drove the car again at Santa Barbara a week later. Max Balchowsky collection.

Above: Max Balchowsky pushing Art Evans' Gilbert IndyCar after a breakdown at Willow Springs in 1985. Max was always right there when help was needed. Photograph by Ginny Dixon. *Left:* Max Balchowsky in 1990 at my home in Redondo Beach. Photograph by the author.

and Ina could not improve Old Yeller's reliability. It was the same story for all the specials; they were prone to break, and that's what makes the Balchowskys' results so incredible!

Sadly, Ina fell ill and passed away on September 16, 1986, at age 54. A devastated Max shut down Hollywood Motors and sold off the cars and equipment. He stayed involved in the racing world helping people that had his cars. Max died unexpectedly on August 30, 1998, at age 74 while attending a reunion in his native West Virginia.

In the early nineties the beat-up old dog was adopted by a loving foster father named Dr. Ernie Nagamatsu. Ernie rejuvenated and groomed Old Yeller II back to its youthful glory and showed it off to the world. The Cinderella dog from the scrapyards of California has been an honored guest in England at Lord Marsh's Goodwood Festival of Speed and at major events around the world.

23

Dan Gurney

A number of those among us stood head and shoulders above all the others during the Golden Age of Autosports. Juan Fangio, Stirling Moss, Carroll Shelby, John Fitch, Dan Gurney and Phil Hill immediately come to mind. But only one among that exalted group was proposed for president of the United States: Daniel Sexton Gurney. All-American boy was the perfect sobriquet for the tall, handsome race driver with the wry grin. Of course, it was all in fun, but I seem to remember unbounded enthusiasm among young ladies of the time. Dan's All American Racers is the only U.S. organization to build and campaign cars that have won in Formula One, CART, USAC and sports cars.

Born in 1931, Dan barely missed being a member of the Greatest Generation. He is a member of what some have called the Silent Generation. It consists of those born in the 1930s and early 1940s. They are the last generation, climbing out of the Depression, who can remember World War II and its impact, which rattled the structure of their daily lives for years.

It seemed as if Dan could do anything and everything. As a driver, he won in virtually every category: Formula One, IndyCars, NASCAR, Can-Am, Trans-Am and World Championship sports car events. He even drove a car he himself created to a Formula One victory, the famed Gurney Eagle with a Gurney Weslake V12 engine. Not content with that, he constructed race-winning IndyCars and was a team owner.

What may not be so widely known is how Dan got started. He was born in Port Jefferson on Long Island, New York, on April 13, 1931. His father—John R. Gurney—was a well-known singer, a star of the Metropolitan Opera Company. His mother—Roma Sexton—was an art teacher and painter. Dan went to Manhasset High School on Long Island, where he majored in hot rodding with his self-built 1933 Ford Roadster. He said, "It was the only thing possible to do on a shoestring, as you put a car together from junkyard parts."

His father retired in 1947. A few days after Dan graduated from high school in 1948, the family moved to Riverside, California, where his parents had purchased a ranch with citrus and avocado groves. Following his mother and father in their 1948 Pontiac station wagon, Dan and his sister drove across the United States on Route 66 in Dan's 1940 Ford. As soon as he arrived, he traded it for a chopped and channeled 1932 Ford coupe with a flathead V8. A succession of rods followed, and Dan indulged in that great California pastime: street racing. His first legal race was in 1950 at Bonneville in a 1935 Ford "zeet-back" sedan. He did 138 mph at the Bonneville Salt Flats. In the meantime, Dan continued his education at Menlo Junior College.

But just as he graduated, an unpleasantness arose in Korea. In late 1951, Dan was accepted into the U.S. Air Force Air Cadet program. He was told to report to Randolph Field in Texas to begin testing to become a pilot. Actually, he wanted to be a fighter pilot. A problem arose when Dan's mother told the Air Force that he was married. "That washed me out," he said. "Air Cadets were not allowed to be married during pilot training."

Rather than be drafted, Dan enlisted in the Army and went on active duty on October 16, 1952. It was a two-year commitment at that time. He had basic training at Fort Ord and advanced training at Fort Bliss. He became a gun mechanic for anti-aircraft cannons. Next, he was sent to Korea and served on the B Battery of the 78th AAA Gun Battalion that protected the K-13 air base near Suwon.

While there, he was promoted to corporal and had his own Jeep. Driving the Jeep, Dan would travel to other battalions to trade parts and other components. Three months after he arrived in Korea, a ceasefire was declared and all the fighting stopped. Target practice and shooting at what they called "Bed Check Charlie," an enemy aircraft that flew over their base at night, was the only action Dan saw firing his 90 mm anti-aircraft

Dan was a gun mechanic on an anti-aircraft cannon in Korea. Dan Gurney collection.

cannon. The 90 mm M1 fired 25 3.5-inch explosive projectiles per minute. It was our answer to the infamous German 88. It could fire a shell 16 miles horizontally or 40,000 feet vertically. After two years of service, Dan was discharged in September 1954.

Afterwards, Dan returned to Riverside and, as a result of buying a Triumph TR2 with his mustering-out pay, gravitated towards the sports car scene. His first race was at Torrey Pines on October 23, 1955. Even though he had entered the TR2 as a production car, he ran in the one-hour main event for modified cars over 1500cc. Bill Murphy won Dan's race, followed by Chuck Daigh and Jack McAfee. Dan finished two laps behind the three in tenth overall and third in Class E. He ran the TR2 again at Palm Springs in December but had a problem when he hit a hay bale trying to avoid Bruce Kessler. Afterwards he said, with his signature wry grin, "I guess I should have hit Bruce."

In 1956, Dan bought a 1600cc Porsche Super Speedster in which he ran a number of races. In racing lore they say you can't beat cubic inches in an engine or seat time for a driver. Dan and his best friend, Skip Hudson, would lay out a course in the hills above the Corona orange groves and clock each other. At local races, they both ran up front from the beginning. On June 23 at Pomona, he was second overall in the race for production cars 1500cc to 2700cc. Second was a first-rate performance, in that his competitors were all in cars over two liters. The next day—Sunday—he was sixth overall and first in Class E. The Sunday event was for big-bore production cars and included 300SLs, Corvettes and Jaguars. Again, this was an excellent result considering the competition. At Santa Maria on July 8, he scored another class win, and later that month Dan had his first overall win at Montgomery Field, just north of San Diego. At Paramount Ranch in November he failed to finish owing to a broken clutch cable. Of an incident at Paramount, Dan said, "When you know you're in deep trouble, your hair stands on end, even under a helmet—and mine did! That course was dangerous, even by the standards of the time."

The following year Dan graduated to driving other people's cars. On May 18 at Santa Barbara, he drove Aussie star E. F. (Robbie) Robinson's Lancia Aurelia in the big-bore production race. Robbie told Dan that he had potential. At the very first race at Riverside in September 1957, Dan drove a Corvette owned by Cal Bailey to first overall in the big-bore production race. This was a sensational win, not only because it was his first time out in a Corvette but also because of the stiff competition from much more experienced drivers. Moved up to the main event, he took the Corvette to sixth overall. This was a creditable result in that the event had mostly Ferraris and Maseratis. Dan's was the first production car. He was clocked at 133.13 mph down Riverside's back straight.

By then, Dan had come to the attention of Frank Arciero, who fielded Ferraris for up-and-comers. Arciero entered Dan in the November 17 SCCA National at Riverside in his potent 4.9 Ferrari. A host of hot dogs were there, including Carroll Shelby, Masten Gregory and Jim Hall in Maseratis, Jack McAfee in a 3.5 Ferrari, Walt Hansgen in a D-Type Jaguar and Richie Ginther in another 4.9. At the start, Shelby, Hansgen and Gregory led off, but Dan suddenly passed Gregory and Hansgen, Shelby spun and Dan was in the lead. Towards the end, Shelby managed to pass Dan, and that's the way it ended. At the checkered flag, Dan was only five seconds behind Shelby, who had set a new course record. The big 4.9 didn't drive like a Porsche. Dan had worn a hole in his glove and blistered his hand. Dan's first big win was at Paramount Ranch on December 8, 1957, where he won the main event in the Arciero 4.9. Dan went on to score 14 overall sports car wins in Southern California. A new star had burst onto the scene.

In 1958, Dan hit the big time driving for Luigi Chinetti's North American Racing Team at Le Mans along with Bruce Kessler in a Ferrari 250 Testa Rossa. They were running fourth overall in the seventh hour when Jean-Marie Brousselet crashed in a Jaguar, causing Bruce to run into the D-Type and take out the Ferrari.

Next, Dan drove a Ferrari at the Reims 12 Hour with Andre Guelfi. While they failed to finish, Dan impressed Enzo Ferrari enough to land a contract for the 1959 season. In 1959, he and Jean Behra raced at Le Mans for Ferrari in a 250 TR. Also, that year, Dan and Chuck Daigh, together with Phil Hill and Olivier Gendebien, won the 12 Hours of Sebring. Dan drove Formula One for Ferrari in 1959 finishing second, third and fourth in four Grand Prix races, quite a record for a newcomer.

Formula One rules were changed in 1961, so Dan changed to the factory Porsche team. During that year, he scored one second and three third places. The next year,

Dan Gurney in a Ferrari leading the first lap of the main event at Pomona in March 1959, followed by Max Balchowsky in Ole Yeller (70). Dan Gurney collection.

Dan (left) with his parents, Roma and John, in 1962. Dan Gurney collection.

Porsche built a car with a more powerful eight-cylinder engine. Dan won the French Grand Prix plus a non-championship Formula One race in Germany. Porsche dropped out of Formula One competition after 1962. While racing with Porsche, Dan met the team public relations officer, Evi Butz. They met at Porsche and were married seven years later.

In 1963, Jack Brabham hired Dan to drive for the Brabham Racing Organization. The team raced cars designed and built by Brabham himself. Dan won the Formula One race at Rouen in 1964. During his time with Brabham, Dan had two wins in 1964 and stood on the podium (meaning he had won first, second or third) ten times.

In NASCAR competition, Dan ran 16 races over a ten-year period. He won 5, had 8 top tens and 10 pole positions. He won the 1963 Riverside 500 for Holman-Moody and then the 1964, 1965, 1966 and 1968 races for the Wood Brothers. Dan's 5 wins were an all-time record at Riverside.

In 1965, Dan Gurney and Carroll Shelby formed the All American Racers team. Not only that, Dan raced for Shelby American and was second at Daytona in 1966, and then there was the big one when he and co-driver A. J. Foyt won the 1967 24 Hours of Le Mans.

Dan, however, had set the goal of winning the Formula One World Championship

Gurney, in Carroll Shelby's Cobra, won the three-hour race at Riverside in October 1963.

in an American car. So he and his crew at All American Racers in Riverside, California, designed and built the Eagle. By that time, Shelby had left, and Dan was all on his own and formed a team he called the Anglo American Racers to campaign the Eagle in Formula One. He wanted to use the Weslake V12 engine, but it was not ready for the start of the 1966 season. So he installed an outdated four-cylinder 2.7 liter Coventry-Climax and used it five times; the best he could do with it was a fifth at Reims.

The debut of the Gurney Eagle with the Weslake engine took place in September 1966 at Monza. For American competition, the Eagle used a larger Ford V8 engine. In March 1967, Dan won a non-championship Formula One at Brands Hatch, England. But the big win was on June 18, 1967, when Dan won the Belgian Grand Prix. It was a historic victory for an American to win a Formula One Grand Prix in an American car. The end of that season marked the end of Dan's Formula One effort.

In Formula One, Dan started 88 races, garnered 3 pole positions, had 4 wins and stood on the podium 19 times. From 1959 through 1970, he accumulated 132 World Championship points.

On November 26, 1967, Dan Gurney won the USAC IndyCar race at Riverside driving his Eagle. Two months later, in January 1968, he won the USAC event at Mosport, and the following year, 1969, at Indianapolis Raceway Park. At Brainerd in

Gurney (holding bottle) and A.J. Foyt celebrating winning Le Mans in 1967. Both photographs, Dan Gurney collection.

September he won again and then, for the last time with USAC, he was first at Sears Point on August 4, 1970.

After winning two SCCA races, Dan retired from racing after 1970. In IndyCar racing, out of 28 starts, he won 10 pole positions, had 7 wins, 4 seconds and 5 third places at the wheel of one of his own Eagles. In 1969 and 1970, he was second at Indianapolis. He wound up with 3 Can-Am wins, 5 NASCAR wins, and 1 Trans-Am.

In total, Dan raced in 312 events in 20 countries driving 25 makes of cars, winning 51 of them. In total, he won 4 Grands Prix, 7 IndyCar events, 5 NASCAR races, and 3 Can-Ams and had wins at Daytona, Sebring, the Nürburgring, Le Mans and a class victory at the Targa Florio.

Above: Dan and Evi. Dan Gurney collection. *Left:* Dan didn't like this shot of himself, but Evi did. Photograph by the author.

Dan has been a member of the Screen Actors Guild since 1965. He appeared in *Winning*, *A Man and a Woman* and *Grand Prix* as well as a number of Toyota commercials. He is one of the founders of the Long Beach Grand Prix. His swan song was participating at the Long Beach Grand Prix from 1980 through 1991 in a preliminary event called the Toyota Pro/Celebrity Race. He won it a number of times.

After his retirement from Formula One, Dan assumed his career as a car maker and team owner full time. He was the chairman and CEO of All

23. Dan Gurney

Dan with his Formula One–winning Eagle outside the Cunningham Museum in Costa Mesa, California, in 2001. Dan Gurney collection.

American Racers until his son, Justin, took over as CEO in 2011. The team won 78 races, including the Indy 500, Sebring and Daytona. Teams that have bought Eagles have won three 500s and three championships.

On a personal note, in 1985 I organized a Vintage Formula One race on the downtown streets of Palm Springs. Dan was one of the first who agreed to help me. Dan was there; he had taken his Formula One winning Gurney Weslake Eagle out of the Cunningham Museum, and he prepared it and raced it himself for the last time. He was the sensation of the weekend.

Dan Gurney was inducted into the International Motorsports Hall of Fame in 1990, also into the Motorsports Hall of Fame of America, the Sebring International Raceway Hall of Fame and the West Coast Stock Car Hall of Fame.

Today, All American Racers is well known and a respected carbon-composite factory run by Justin, with 180 employees. Among other projects, AAR is building the landing gear for Elon Musk's space rockets as well as projects for the military and Tesla.

Dan and his wife, the former Porsche press officer Evi Butz, lived in Newport Beach, California. They had two sons. Dan had eight children and four grandchildren from his first marriage. He enjoyed reading history, old movies, opera, cigars and motorcycling.

Dan Gurney enjoyed a considerable international fan base and was well liked within the motor racing industry. Not content with a quiet retirement, Dan designed and developed a unique motorcycle, the Gurney Alligator, that has to be seen to be believed.

Daniel Sexton Gurney died on Sunday, January 13, 2018, from complications due to pneumonia with his wife, Evi, at his side. He was 86 years old.

Epilogue

Over time, the men and women of the Greatest Generation have left us.

The decade following the "Fabulous Fifties" has been called "the Sensational Sixties." It was markedly different from the fifties. Road racing in the United States during the fifties was, for the most part, a hobby indulged in by amateur enthusiasts. The sixties, however, was marked by the coming of the professionals.

The decade of the sixties is called Sensational and most of the 23 in this book were there. The sixties were marked by hugely popular professional series: The U.S. Road Racing Championship (USRRC), the Can-Am (the Canadian-American Challenge) and the Trans Am (small sedan series). The most unusual of all was the Can-Am. That series had almost no rules except the cars had to be sports cars. Engines and body styles saw radical changes. These series were broadly popular, not only among paying spectators but also as televised events. After the sixties, these series diminished in popularity as a flood of new attractions came on the scene and America's love affair with the automobile cooled. There was never anything before or afterwards like the Fabulous Fifties and the Sensational Sixties. The post-war period up until early in the seventies has been named the "Golden Age of Speed" by Sam Posey. He meant, I think, "in the U.S."

All twenty-three of those profiled in this book left an indelible mark on racing in one way or another that can't be erased. All of them served on active duty during WWII, or in Korea, as is the case with Dan Gurney. Each of those described in this book were friends of mine, some very close. Quite obviously, there were many more of our Greatest Generation who participated in racing after their return from war. This book doesn't pretend to provide an exhaustive list; just twenty-three of my good friends. When I looked over their records, I was amazed. A total of fourteen lived to over 80 years of age while two lived over 90. This has to say something about their generation. The average expectancy for those born in 1920 is 53.5. Most of the twenty-three lived full lives and left behind a lasting legacy of accomplishments.

The heroes featured in this book, including the women, used skills, both physical and mental, acquired in wartime to improve our mobility.

World War II changed much of the world. War became mechanized, particularly with the importance of air power. It ushered in weapons of mass destruction, most notably the atomic bomb. Tanks and other motorized vehicles replaced horses.

Motorsports experienced significant changes too. Without the post-war influx of MGs in the U.S., car racing would be very different. In fact, amateur road racing became as important a sport as professional oval-track racing. Those people described in this book, as well as others like them, had an impact on the sport as well as the automobiles.

Before road racing became popular, American auto racing focused on horsepower, oval track and straightaway speed. Suspensions and chassis were primitive. Road racing brought the need for agility, good brakes, and the ability to run fast on rough and twisty roads. The modern family sedan is capable of a comfortable 80 mph on less than perfect roads.

World War II radically changed the United States. Pre-war, our military was pitifully small. Afterwards, America grew to be a dominant world power. The importance of women in the workplace increased because "Rosie the Riveter" on assembly lines had replaced the men who had gone to war. Mass production became the norm for industry. Populations moved to the cities from the countryside as ever large machines replaced farm workers.

As an intellectual exercise, try to imagine what the world would be like if World War II had never taken place.

Bibliography

Brabham, Sir Jack, with Doug Nye. *The Jack Brabham Story*. St. Paul, MN: Motorbooks International, 2004.
Considine, Tim. *American Grand Prix Racing: A Century of Drivers & Cars*. Osceola, WI: MBI, 1997.
Davis, Mary. *Her Way!* Redondo Beach, CA: Self-published, 2012.
Evans, Art. *The Amazing Life of John Cooper Fitch*. Hudson, WI: Enthusiast Books, 2014.
Evans, Art. *Carroll Shelby: A Collection of My Favorite Racing Photos*. Forest Lake, MN: CarTech, 2016.
Evans, Art. *Race Legends of the Fabulous Fifties*. Redondo Beach, CA: Photo Data Research, 2003.
Finn, Joel E. *Caribbean Capers*. New Milford, CT: Garnet Hill Publishing, 2010.
Fitch, John. *Adventure on Wheels*. New York: G. P. Putnam's Sons, 1956.
Georgano, G. N. *The Encyclopedia of Motor Sport*. New York: Viking Press, 1971.
Goodwin, Carl. *They Started in MGs: Profiles of Sports Car Racers of the 1950s*. Jefferson, NC: McFarland, 2011.
Jones, Parnelli. *As a Matter of Fact, I Am Parnelli Jones*. Newburyport, MA: Coastal, 2012.
Madigan, Tom. *Boss: The Bill Stroppe Story*. Burbank, CA: Darwin Publications, 1984.
McCarthy, Todd. *Fast Women: The Legendary Ladies of Racing*. New York: Miramax Books/Hyperion, 2007.
O'Leary, Mike. *Rodger Ward: Superstar of American Racing's Golden Age*. St. Paul, MN: Motorbooks, 2006.
Pollack, Bill. *Red Wheels and White Sidewalls: Confessions of an Allard Racer*. Carpinteria, CA: Brown Fox Books, 2004.
Schultz, Tom. *Road America: Five Decades of Racing at Elkhart Lake*. Indianapolis, IN: Beeman Jorgensen, 1999.
Stone, Matt. *McQueen's Machines: The Cars and Bikes of a Hollywood Icon*. Indianapolis, IN: Beeman Jorgensen, 1999.
Wyss, Wallace A. *Shelby: The Man, the Cars, the Legend*. Hudson, WI: Iconografix.
Zimmermann, John. *Dan Gurney's Eagle Racing Cars*. Phoenix, AZ: David Bull Publishing, 2007.

Websites

Ancestry.com
DestroyerHistory.org
HistoricRacing.com
RacingSportsCars.com
Wikipedia.com

Index

Numbers in *bold italics* indicate pages with illustrations

AAA National Stock Car Championship 2, 3, 109, 118, 120
ABC's *Wide World of Sports* for NASCAR 112
Abecassis, George 3
AC Cars 94
Adams, Neile *see* McQueen, Neile
Adler, Stella 125
Agajanian, J.C. 143
Aintree, England 91
Alameda Naval Air Station 131
All American Racers 175, 179, 180, 183
Amon, Chris 63, 96
Andersen, Arthur 172
Andretti, Mario 24, 32, 137
Anglo American Racers 180
Annis, Casey 22
Anschluss 100
Arciero, Frank 177
Argentine Grand Prix 5, 11, 91
Arkus-Duntov, Zora 11, 40
Ascot Raceway 130, 151
Atsugi Airfield Japan 139
Atwater, Clem 61
Australian Air Force 111
Auto Racing All-American Team Banquet 140
Avandaro, Mexico 104
Aviation Mechanics School 159

Bahamas Speed Week 106
Bailey, Cal 177
Baja California Race 112; *see also* La Carrera Classic
Balboa Park 114
Balboa Stadium 107

Balchowsky, Caspar 167, 168
Balchowsky, Ina Wilson 168, ***169***, 172
Balchowsky, Max Ernest v, 1, 3, 77, 143, ***169-171, 173-174***, 178
ball turret 167
Barber, Dick 23, 26
Barlow, Roger 80, 101
Barnes, Tom 145, 146
Battle of the Bulge 143
Bay Cities National Bank 33
Baylor University Hospital 99
Bean, Rod v
Beaufort, Count Carel de 14, ***18***
Beazley, John 59
Behra, Jean 3, 178
Belgian Grand Prix 143, 180
Belond Exhaust Special 121
Belond, Sandy 168
Berg, Ken 14
Berkeley Gazette 137
Berman, Larry v, 12, 13
Bessemyer, Jay 143
Beverly Hills, California 106, 129
Beverly Wilshire Hotel 129
Bigelow, Joe 102
Bondurant, Bob 22, 38, 96, 133, 135, 173
Bonneville 91
Bonnier, Jo 3
Boyington, Greg "Pappy" 49
Brabham, Sir Jack 62, 108, 111, 114, 142, 159, 179
Brando, Maralon 169
Briney, Max 143
Bristol Aeroplane Company 94

British Aluminium Company 47
Brock, Pete 94
Brokaw, Tom 1
Brousselet, Jean-Marie 178
Brown, Charles 90
Bryan, Jimmy 155
Buchanan, George 43
Bucknam, Ronnie ***63***, 126, 173
Buell, Temple 91
Bullitt 124, 170
USS *Bunker Hill* 22
Butz, Evi *see* Gurney, Evi

Caddo Mills Texas Race 89, 90
Cahier, Bernard v
California Junior Boys Republic, Chino 125
California Roadster Association 42
California Sports Car Club 2, 27, 50, 60, 69, 70, 73, 79, 80, 85, 100, 101, 132, 135
Callicult, Earl 126
Camoradi Team 91
Camp Callan 100
Can-Am Racing 23, 175, 185
Cane, Arnie 146, ***149***
Caracciola, Rudi 11
Carburetion Day 117
Carburetor Equipment Company 129
Carrell Speedway 50, 101, 143, 152, 153
La Carrera Classic 153
Carrera Panamericana 10, 42, 43, 50, 43, 113, 143, 155
Carroll Shelby Children's Foundation 99
Carroll Shelby Hall 1, 2, 3, 17,

189

Index

18, *32*, 40, 57, 62, 65, 84, ***88-89***, ***92-93***, ***96-98***, 107, 118, ***126***, 142, 147, 159, 162, 172, ***173***, 175, 178, 179, 180; in Africa 97; family 99; other books by Art Evans 99; other business ventures 97
Carrozzeria Scaglietti Design Team 93
Carstens, Tom 79, 82, 83, 168
CART Racing 175
Carter, Duane 18
USS *Casco* 151, 152
Caterpillar Tractor Company *see* Holt Brothers
Central Intelligence Agency (CIA) 101, 131
Chamberlain, Beverly 42, 46
Chamberlain, Jamie v, 42, 43, 45, 46
Chamberlain, Jay Clifford v, 1, 2, ***42-43***, ***45-47***, ***69***, 135, 163, 172
Chamberlain, Jody 46
Chamberlain, Marion 46
Chandler Family 140
Chapman, Colin 41, 44, 47, 48, 159, 163
Charisse, Cyd 121
Cherryholme, Roy 91
Chicago Sportsman's Trophy 116
Child, Julia 131
Chinetti, Luigi 15, 178
Chitwood, Joie 120
Chrysler Proving Grounds, Michigan 118
Churchill, Winston 167
Clark, Jimmy 48, 164
Cleye, Rudy 67
Coach & Horses Restaurant 131
Cobras 18, 19, 94, 95, 96, 97, 180
Coburn, James 170
Cogan, Kevin 114
Cole, Ed 11, 93
Cole, Tom 10
Competition Body Shop 168
Competition Motors 61, 101, 102
Composite Automobile Research 113
Constantine, George 111
Coogan, Bobby 82
Cooper, John 10, 111, 160
Coppel, Al ***160***
Corband, Richard 75
Corregidor, Fortress 15, 16, 41, 42, 129, 167

Cramer, Peyton ***98***
Crawford, Ray 155
Crow, Jim 65
Cuba 17, 92
Cummings, Ron v
Cunningham, Briggs 2, 10, 19
Cunningham, Rug 114
Cunningham Museum 183
Czech Air Force 72
Czechoslovak 250 cc Championship 72

Dai Ichi Building, Tokyo 139
Daigh, Charles George 3, 51, 111, 129, ***144-148***, 155, 177, 178; with Bronze Star 142
Daigh, Daniel 149
Daigh, Denise 149
Daigh, Doris (Wingard) 149
Davis, Mary v, ***28-33***, 129, ***133***, ***134***, 135
Dean, James 169, 170
Deen, Dorothy 171, 172
Denny, Reginald 168
Destroyer Squadron 21 41
Devin, Gene 35
Devin, Mildred (Middie) 38, 40
Devin, William Elbert ***36-40***
Devin Enterprises 36, 37
Dixon, Ginny v, 106, 174
Dixon, John v, 55, 118
D'Olivo, Bob v
Doretti 171, 172
Douglas Aircraft 35
Drake, Bob 27, ***28***, 70, 173

Eagle Squadron 7
Earle, Steve 77, 83
Economaki, Chris 111
Ecurie Excelsior Team 44
Edelbrock, Vic 108
Edgar, John 2, 67, 69, 73, 80, 91, 92, 173
Edwards, Sterling 80, 82
Edwards Air Force Base 115, 122
82nd Airborne Division 143
11th Airborne Division 15
Ellico, Ron 67
Emery, Paul 58
Espiritu Santo 49
Estes, Bob 62, 155
Evans, Art 37, ***132***, 133, 153, 174; books 84, 99
Evans, Art, Sr. ***39***, ***65***
Evans, Dave (Ford) 94
Evans, David 19, 99
Evans, Robb ***37***
Evans Industries 37, 39, 172

Fabulous Fifties 1, 85, 185
Fabulous Fifties' Lifetime Achievement Award 46
Fangio, Juan 10, 17, 62, 92, 111, 133, 175
Farragut, Idaho 41, 49
Faulkner, Walt 155
Felton, Gene 114
Ferrari, Enzo 100, 178
Ferrari Representatives of California 105
FIA (Federation International Automobile) 2, 3, 94-96, 109
Fields, Jeanne *see* Shelby, Jeanne
Firestone Tire and Rubber Company test car 118
Fitch, Elizabeth 11, 14
Fitch, John Cooper v, 1, 2, ***6-7***, ***9***, ***11-14***, 91, 111, 118, 160, 162, 175; family 14; as prisoner of war 8; on ME 262 shot down 7
Fitch Inertial Barriers 12, 13
517th Parachute Infantry Combat Team 142, 143
503rd Parachute Regimental Combat Team 15, 16, 42
Flamingo Hotel & Casino 168
Follmer, George 75
Ford, Benson 143, 153
Ford, Henry, II 63, 143
Ford Motor Company 18, 64, 94, 96, 98, 108, 128, 151, 153
Formula Libre Event 111
Formula One 175, 183
Fort Benning, Georgia 15
Foyt, A.J. 111, 179, ***181***
Frere, Paul 91
Friedman, Dave v, 153, 154

Gazzara, Ben 126
Geddes, Ray 94
Gendebien, Olivier 178
German Home Guard 8
Gilbert, Howard 121
Gilmore Stadium 108, 115, 130, 132, 151
Ginther, Richie 3, 75, 104, 105, 177
Glick, Shavenau ***138-140***; and awards 141; family 141; with *Pasadena Star News, Los Angeles Mirror, Los Angeles Times* 139
Golden Age of Racing 107, 185
Golden Gate Park 82, 159, 160
Golden Globe Award 124
Goodyear Racing tires 94

Gough, Phil, Sr. 61
Gough Industries 59
Grand Central Airport, Glendale 79, 162, 172
Grand Prix Restaurant *31*
Grant, Jerry 114
Greatest Generation 1
Gregory, Masten 15, 111, 177
Grossman, Bob 17
Guadalcanal Battle 22, 41, 49
Guasti, Secondo 101
Guelfi, Andre 178
Guiberson, Allen 91, 92
Gurney, Daniel Sexton 3, 40, 57, 76, 96, 135, 142, 147, 173, *175-184*
Gurney, Evi (Butz) 179, *182*, 183, 184
Gurney, John R. 175, *179*
Gurney, Justin 183
Gurney, Roma Sexton *179*
Gurney Alligator Motorcycle 184

Haas, Carl 24, *25*
Hall, Art 151, 153
Hall, Jim 93, 177
Hallett, Burton 157
Hallett, Luanne *see* Stroppe, Luanne
Hamburger (Hammy) family 130
Hamilton, Duncan 91
Hanks, Alice v, 116, 118, *122*
Hanks, Samuel Dwight 7, 107, *115-117, 119-122*, 155, 168
Hansgen, Walt 147, 177
Harrah, Bill 168
Hart, John 104
Hauser, Eric 172
Hawthorn, Mike 47
Haywood, Hurley 75
Healey, Donald 91
Hedrick, Alice *see* Hanks, Alice
Hefley, Mary 132; *see also* O'Connor, Mary
Hefner, Hugh 135
Hill, Graham 164
Hill, Phil 3, *19*, 40, *52*, 57, 76, 80, 83, 92, 95, 104, *147*, 152, 153, 175, 178
Hirohito, Emperor 138, 170
Hitler, Adolf 100
Hoffman, Max 73, 84
Hole in the Wall Gang 25
Hollywood High School 130
Hollywood Motors 168, 170
Holman, Jake 127, 170

Holt Brothers 158; *see also* Caterpillar
Hooper, Doug 95
Hornburg, Charles 43
Hudson, Skip *96*, 177
Hughes, Howard 172
Hugus, Edward James *1, 16-20*, 42, 94, 95, 129
Hulman, Tony 121
Hulme, Denny 63, 96
Hurlock, Charles 94
Hutcherson, Dick 63

Iacocca, Lee 97
Ickx, Jackie 75
Iglesias, Davalos 155
Indianapolis Motor Speedway 5, 109, 111, 112, 115, 116, 121, 134, 141
Indianapolis Motor Speedway Radio Network 112
Indianapolis Raceway Park 180
IndyCar Racing 175, 181
Ireland, Innes 163

Jaguar factory 68
James P. Chapman Award *140*
Japan, Occupation of 17, 138
Jeffers, Hipolita 129
Jeffers, Jack V. 129
Jeffers, Virginia Marie *see* Sims, Virginia
Jenkinson, Denis 11
Johncock, Gordon 114
Johnson, Ham 5
Jones, Harry 56
Jones, Myra 73
Jones, Parnelli *154*, 155, 159
Jones, Spike 118
Jopp, Peter *17*, 19, *96*
Jordan, Davey 75, 77
Jordan, Norma 77
Justice Brothers' Shav Glick Award 141

Kellogg, Ron v
Kennedy, Bobby 9
Kennedy, Joe 9
Kennedy, John F. 9, 10
Kennedy, Kathleen 8, 9, 10
Kennedy, Rose *9*
Kennedy, Teddy 9
Kessler, Bruce 142, 177, 178
Kiekhaefer, Carl 10
Kindelberger, James Howard "Dutch" 159
King of England 10
Kiwanis Club 3
Klein, Don 14
Knight, Michael 140

Korean War 176
Krause, Bill 53, 95, 173
Kuhn, Allen v
Kunming China 131, 167
Kunstle, John *53*
Kurtis, Frank 143, 153, 168, 172

Lackland Air Force Base 88
Laguna Seca 54, 55, 83, 156, 162, 163
Lake Geneva 106
Laughlin, Gary 93
Laughlin Field Training Command, Texas 79
LeMay, General Curtis 68
Levegh, Pierre 12
Lightfoot, Dylan v
Lime Rock Park 12, 26, 108, 111
Littlejohn, Anna Marie *see* Polak, Anna Marie
Livingstone, Frank "Duffy" 42, 172
Lockheed Aircraft 117
Loftin, Carey 170
Long Island City Raceway 126
Los Angeles Coliseum 118
Los Angeles Times Grand Prix 3, 95, 115, 147, 159
Lotus Cars Company 47, 48
Lovely, Gerard Carlton "Pete" 158, *160-165*
Lovely, Mildred 158
Lovely, Nevele 165
Lovely, Patricia *161*
Lowe, Marion 143
Lozano, Ignacio "Nacho" 43; with *La Opinion* 44
Lubin, Joe 27, *28*
Lucas, Taylor 101
Luftwaffe 7
Lumbleau School of Real Estate 27
Luzon Philippines 15
Lynch, Michael: *American Sports Car Racing in the 1950s* 102

MacAllister, Chris 164
MacArthur, Gen. Arthur 138
MacArthur, Gen. Douglas 138
MacDill Air Force Base 17
MacDonald, Dave 52, 95, *96*, 111, 159, 172
MacGraw, Ali 128
MacGregor, Malcolm 37
MacKay-Fraser, Herbert 41, 44, *45*
Mann, Harry 133
Manney, Henry 35
Mansell, Nigel 24

Index

Mantz, Johnny 152, 155
March Field 103, 170
Marine Corps Women's Reserve 27
McAfee, Ernie 35, 50, 80
McAfee, Gerry 56
McAfee, Jack Ernest **29**, **50-55**, 73, **74**, 75, 77, 104, 121, **162**, 177
McAfee, Mimi 56
McAfee, Pat **52**
McAfee, Rex v, 55, 56
McCluskey, Mike 98
McLaren, Bruce 62, 63, 96, 147, 159
McQueen, Barbara (Minty) 128
McQueen, Chad 126
McQueen, Neile (Adams) 126
McQueen, Terrence Stephen 68, 69, **126-128**, 170; in movies 124, 126, 127, 128
McQueen, Terry Leslie 126
Mears, Roger 114
Meisner, Sanford 125
Menasco Manufacturing 131
Mercedes-Benz Team 10
Mercury cars 155
Merle Norman Cosmetics 85
Mexican Road Race 54, 143
Meyer, Louise 120
Michelmore, D.D. 70
Mile Square Orange County California 122
Miles, Kenneth Henry 1, **39**, 44, **58-61**, **63-65**, **69**, 73, **74**, 75, 95, **96**, 102, 103, 115, 122, 135, 143, 159
Miles, Mollie 57, 58, **61**, 64, 65
Miles, Peter v, 65
Mille Miglia 10, 11
Miller Engines, Harry 108, 113, 120, 129
Minh, Ho Chi 167
Mintner, Milt 75, 77
Minty, Barbara *see* McQueen, Barbara
USS *Missouri* 139
Mobilgas Economy Run 29, 67, **133**, **134**, 154
Monroe, Marilyn 79
Monroe Shock Absorbers 122
Monte Carlo Rally 10
Monterey Historics 14, 19, 39, **40**, 46, 54, 83, 157, 165
Monza, Italy 62
Moon, Dean 94
Morton, John 75, 77, 114
Mosher, Samuel B. 150, 151

Moss, Sir Stirling 10, 14, 76, 164, 175
Moss, Susie 14
Motorsports Hall of Fame 14, 137, 141
Muroc Dry Lake 115, 130, 151
Murphy, Bill 121, **145**, 177
Musk, Elon 183

Nagamatsu, Dr. Ernie v, 174
NASCAR 24, 175, 179, 181
Nassau Trophy 44, 147
Nation, Fred 141
National Cash Register (NCR) 118
National Championship Air Races 122
Nehamkin, Lester v, 146
Nethercutt, Jack 163
Nethercutt Auto Museum 168
Newman, Paul Leonard 1, **22-25**, 126, 127; in Guinness Book of World Records 23; in movies 21-23
Newman-Haas Team 24
Newman-Wachs Racing 23
Newman's Own 25
Nichels, Ray 118
Nichino, Kozo 151
USS *Nicholas* 41, 42
North American Aviation 159
North American Racing Team 250GT (NART) 117, 178

Oakes, Danny 188
O'Connor, Mary 132, 135; *see also* Hefley, Mary
Off-Road Motorsports Hall of Fame 156
Offenhauser engines, Fred 107, 108, 109, 113, 115, 116, 129
Office of Strategic Services (OSS) 131
Okinawa Campaign 22, 152
Olson, Warren 146
One Lap of America 32
Ongais, Danny 32, 75
Ontario Motor Speedway 112, 121
Operation Dragoon/Anvil 129, 142
La Opinion see Lozano, Ignacio "Nacho"
Orr, Jim 36
Orr, Karl 168
Orr, Veda 168
O'Shea, Paul 162, 173
OSS Dixie Mission Deer Team 167

Otto Zipper-Bob Estes Team 62
Owooso Speedway, Michigan 112

Pabst, Augie 17
Pacific Coast Midget Championship 118
Pacific Sports Car Club 50
Palm Springs Road Races 50, 67, 70, 75, 80, 83, 84, 106, 113, 121, 152, 162, 177, 183
Palos Verdes Time Trial 101
Paramount Pictures 131
Paramount Ranch Races 42, 44, 73, 74, 84, 120, 145, 149, 155, 177
Paramount Ranch Remembered 84
Parker, Steve 21
Parkinson, Don 143
Parnell Racing, Reg 3, 109, 112
Parravano, Ron **52**
Parravano, Tony 50, 51, 91, 92
Parsons, Johnny 3, **147**
Patrick, Scooter 77
Patti, Col. Archimedes 167
Patton, Gen. George 8
Pebble Beach 44, 54, 82, 101
Penske, Roger 24, 141, 159
Peron, Evita 10, 11
Peron, Juan 10
Petersen Automotive Museum 14, 94, 106, 149
Peterson, J. Stephen 69, 71
Peterson, James Edward v, **68-69**, **127**
Peterson, Marjorie Steen 67
Philippines Campaign 41, 152
Playboy Mansion 135
Polak, Anna Maria (Littlejohn) **76**, 78
Polak, Jindriska 72, 75
Polak, Vasek 1, 32, 40, 50, **53**, **74**, **76-78**, 106
Polak Imaging Center 78
Pollack, Bobbi 79, 85, 86
Pollack, Jim 80, **81**, 84, 85, 86
Pollack, Leslie 85
Pollack, Mellette 85, 86
Pollack, William Mellette **80-85**, 135, 143, 168
Pomona Fairground Races 60, 69, 70, 73, 105, 120, 177, 178
Porsche, Ferry 100
Porsche four-cam racing engine 62, 72, 73, 75
Porterfield, Andy 39
Portofino Inn 32, 33, 34, 134
Posey, Sam 75, 185

192

Index

Powell, Gladys 172
Prague, Czechoslovakia 72
Presley, Elvis 170
Preston, Tom 34
Pritchard, Margaret 172

Quiet Birdmen, professional race pilots 122, 123

Racing with Mercedes 13
Radio Plane Corporation 169
Rahal, Bobby 24
Randolph Field, Texas 87
Rathmann, Jim 3
Raybestos Brakes 121
Red Wheels and White Sidewalls: Confession of an Allard Racer 85
Redford, Robert 79
Redman, Brian 75, 77
Remington, Phil 146
Reventlow, Lance 3, 94, 146, 172
Reynolds, Burt 32
Richter, Roy 116
Rindt, Jochen 15
Ritch, OCee 37, 38
Riverside International Raceway 62, 64, 66, 67, 68, 75, 94, 95, 109, 112, 121, 133, 163, 172, 175, 177, 179, 180
Riviere, Nicole 136
Riviere, Sacha 136
Road & Track 53, 75
Robinson, E. Forbes "Robbie" 80, 177
Robinson, Jackie 137
Rodriguez, Ricardo 111
Roosevelt, President Franklin Delano 1, 167
Rootes Motors 62
Rose Parade 1962 137
Rosie the Riveter 129
Royal Corps of Electrical & Mechanical Engineers 58
Rubirosa, Porfirio 102
Ruby, Lloyd 62, 63, **64**, 96
Russell, Jane 79
Ruttman, Troy 3, 152, 155

Saab 96 22
Saint, Eva Marie 21
Sakai, Saburo 22
Saks, Eddie 111
Salih, George 121
USS *Samaritan* 152
Sampson, Alden L., II 120
Sampson V16 120
San Diego Automobile Museum 114

San Fernando Valley 168
Sand Pebbles 170
Santa Barbara/Goleta Races 132
Saugus (Bonelli) Stadium 132
Sawyer, George 51
Scarab 146, 147, 172
Scheckter, Jody 75
Schlesser, Jo 96
Schroeder, Gordon 118
Schwarzkopf, Gen. Norman 97
Scott Newman Center 25
Sebring 2, 10–12, 17, 19, 44, 54, 62–64, 67, 91, 92, 96, 111, 112, 127, 147, 160, 163, 164, 178, 181
78th AAA Gun Battalion B Battery 176
Sexton, Roma *see* Gurney, Roma
Sharp Racing Team, Bob 23
Shelby, Cleo 99
Shelby, Jeanne (Fields) **88**, 99
Shelby American Company v, 62, 94, 97, 179
Shelby-Hall Partnership 93
Shelby International 99
Shelby School of High Performance Driving 94
Shell Oil Company 150
Shutes, Betty 73
Signal Gasoline Company 150, 151
Signal Hill 150
Sims, Frances Ann 131, 136
Sims, Frank 130, 136
Sims, Virginia (Ginny) Marie Jeffers v, 29, **33**, 38, **130**, **132-136**; Fastest Woman of the Year Award 133
Sinatra, Frank 21, 127
Sitz, Jim v
Skelton, Betty 29
Skoda factory 72
Smith, Clay 143, 154, 155
Smith, Leah 98
Smith, Tracey v, 63, 64, 96, 98
Sneva, Tom 114
Society of Automotive Engineers (SAE) 13
Soldier Field 116
Southern California Timing Association 130, 168
Sparks, Art 168
Spencer, Lew 95, **96**
Spindler, George 5
Sports Car Club of America (SCCA) 17, 22, 23, 27, 36, 53, 54, 55, 69, 75, 91, 92, 95,

96, 100, 143, 145, 152, 159, 162, 168, 170, 171, 177, 181
Sports Car Journal 31, 67
Sports Illustrated 92
Steen, Marjorie *see* Peterson, Marjorie
Stevenson, Chuck 155
Stillwell, "Vinegar Joe" 167
Stokes, Doug v, 138, **140**
Strasberg Actors' Studio, Lee 22
Stroppe, Ada 150
Stroppe, Bill 53, 120, 143, **153–156**
Stroppe, Claude 150
Stroppe, Debbie v, 157
Stroppe, Helen (Tavasti) 151, 157
Stroppe, Luanne (Hallett) 157
Stroppe, Willie v, 157
Sugarman, Stan 73, 75
Sunbeam Alpines 62
Swendsen, Ted 132, 133
Syme, Doris 141

Tacoma Vintage 112
Tavasti, Helen *see* Stroppe, Helen
Taylor, Elizabeth 21
Technicolor 131
Territorial Army 58
Thayssen, Jorgen 43
Thompson, Carl 78
Thompson, Mickey 111
Thorne, Joel 168
Timanus, John 94
Titus, Jerry 75
Tomaso, Alejandro de 18
Torrance Memorial Hospital 76, 77, 78
Torrey Pines 43, 60, 92, 100, 102, 103, 169, 170, 177
Trans-American Sedan Race 22, 175
Trenton Races 112
Troutman, Dick 145
Troutman-Barnes Special 60, 143, 145, 146
Truman, President Harry 125
24 Hours of Daytona 23, 62, 63, 96, 155, 179
24 Hours of LeMans **3**, **6**, 10, 12, 15–17, 19, 23, 41, 44, 63, 91–93, 96, 97, 128, 147, 163, 178, 181; with crash of 1955 14

Ulmann, Alec 2
United Racing Association 108

Index

United States Automobile Club (USAC) 3, 4, 70, 93, 109, 145, 155, 180, 181
United States Grand Prix for Sports Cars 147
United States Road Racing Association (USRRC) 185
United States Sports Car Club (USSCC) 70
Unser, Bobby 3, 4, 112
Unser Brothers 32

Valentine, Dr. John 68
Van Dyke, Louis *102*
Van Laanen, Dick *61*
VFW Motor City Speedway Championship, Detroit 116
Vichy French 167
Viet Nam 112, 167
Vintage Racecar Magazine 22
Vintage Racing 112, 113, 153, 183
Virginia International Raceway 7, 22
Vogel, Fred 170
Von Dutch Pinstriping 168
Von Neumann, Elinor 80, 100, 102, *104*, 105
Von Neumann, John *1*, *3*, 40, 50, *61*, 62, 75, 77, 80, *101–106*, 162
Von Neumann, Jose 102, 104
Von Neumann, Monica *106*
von Schuschnigg, Chancellor Kurt 100
Vukovich, Bill 152

Waco CG-4A Glider 66
Wagner, Robert *23*
Wallace, Charlie 91
Walters, Phil 2, 10
Ward, Rodger Morris *2*, 91, *108–110*, *112–114*
Ward, Ron 113
Ward, Sherrie 113, 114
Ware, Bob 151
Warner, Dale 132
water injection 7, 117, 118
Watkins Glen 22, 112
Watson, A.J. 111
Wayne, John 129
Weatherly, Joe 69
Wexler, Haskell 170
Wiggins Trade School 49
Wilder, Thornton 21
Wilkens, Ed 88, 89, 90
Williams, Ted 137
Willow Springs Raceway, California 112, 131, 143, 174
Wingard, Doris *see* Daigh, Doris
Wingate, Orde 167
Winning 21, 22, *23*, 182
Witte, Jackie 25
Wolseley Motors 57, 58
Wood, Natalie 79
Woods, Pete 38
Woodward, Joanne 21, 22, *23*, 24
World Manufacturers' Championship 62
Wright-Patterson Field 6, 107, 117, 118
Wyler, John 91

Yates, Brock, Cannonball Run 32
Yeager, Chuck 122
Yedor, Cy 60

Ziegfeld Follies 100
Zipper-Estes Team 62

www.ingramcontent.com/pod-product-compliance
Lightning Source LLC
Chambersburg PA
CBHW081558300426
44116CB00015B/2927